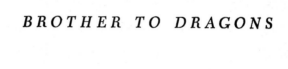

BROTHER TO DRAGONS

Books by ROBERT PENN WARREN

John Brown: The Making of a Martyr
Thirty-six Poems
Eleven Poems on the Same Theme
Night Rider
Selected Poems, 1923–1943
At Heaven's Gate
All the King's Men
The Circus in the Attic
World Enough and Time

BROTHER TO DRAGONS

A Tale in Verse and Voices

BY

ROBERT PENN WARREN

 *RANDOM HOUSE*

Third Printing

Designed by George Salter

Manufactured in the United States of America

To CLEANTH *and* TINKUM BROOKS

An old Indian expressed to Col. Moore great astonishment that white people could live in a country which had been the scene of such conflicts. An old Sac warrior, whom Col. Joseph Hamilton Daviess met in St. Louis in 1800, gave utterance to similar expressions of surprise. Kentucky he said was filled with the ghosts of its slaughtered inhabitants: how could the white man make it his home?

HISTORY OF CHRISTIAN COUNTY, by W. H. Perrin
(Chicago and Louisville, 1884)

. . . when it shake the earth dont be afraid no harm anybody

Letter of Wovoka, the Messiah—Arapaho version.
FOURTEENTH ANNUAL REPORT OF THE BUREAU OF
ETHNOLOGY, Part 2 (Washington, 1893)

For as children tremble and fear everything in the blind darkness, so we in the light sometimes fear what is no more to be feared than the things that children in the dark hold in terror and imagine will come true. This terror, therefore, and darkness of the mind must be dispersed, not by the rays of the sun nor the bright shaft of daylight, but by the aspect and law of nature.

Lucretius: DE RERUM NATURA, III
(*translated by* W. H. D. Rouse)

FOREWORD

Early in the last century, Dr. Charles Lewis, a planter and physician of Albemarle County, Virginia, removed to West Kentucky and established himself on a tract of land not far from the frontier settlements of Smithland and Salem, in what is now Livingston County, upriver from Paducah at the confluence of the Ohio and Cumberland. He took with him his wife and two of his children—two grown sons named Lilburn and Isham—and a number of slaves. On a bluff overlooking the Ohio, he built a house, somewhat grand for the time and place, and quarters for the "people." He called the house Rocky Hill. His wife, Lucy Jefferson Lewis, the sister of Thomas Jefferson, died soon after the removal to Kentucky, and was buried on the bluff, some yards from the house. Charles Lewis now spent little time at Rocky Hill, making a trip to Virginia and leaving Lilburn, with Lilburn's wife and children, and Isham to occupy the house and manage the estate.

On the night of December 15, 1811—the night when the New Madrid earthquake first struck the Mississippi Valley—Lilburn, with the assistance of Isham and in the presence of his Negroes, butchered a slave named George, whose offense had been to break a pitcher prized by the dead mother, Lucy

Lewis. After some months the crime was revealed, and **Lilburn** and Isham were arrested, taken to Salem, then the county seat of Livingston County, and indicted for murder. They were released on bail to await trial, but before the trial, they made an agreement to shoot each other across the grave of their mother. The arrangements miscarried, and Lilburn, with his will in his pocket, fell dying across the grave, and Isham fled to the woods. But Isham was quickly taken, brought to trial, convicted, and sentenced to be hanged. Shortly before the date of execution, however, he broke jail, and despite a heavy reward, was not retaken. For three years he disappears from the record, but when the local militiamen, after service with Andrew Jackson at New Orleans, returned to Livingston County, they reported that they had seen and talked with Isham at the battle and that he had been killed there by a British musket-ball.

I have stayed within the outlines of this record, but have modified details in two respects. First, I have simplified matters where details would clog the action and seemed irrelevant to my theme. For instance, I have dropped Lilburn's children from the account, and I omit the presence of Dr. Lewis in Kentucky in May, 1812,* before Isham's trial. Second, I have un-

---

* Dr. Lewis appears at the proving of Lilburn's will at the May session of the County Court in 1812. I do not know his whereabouts for the preceding months.

dertaken to fill in the gaps of action and motivation, for instance, in the personal story of Laetitia and Lilburn. And I have even invented two characters, though minor characters, Aunt Cat and Laetitia's brother, to serve as certain "voices" that seemed necessary to my theme.

In regard to the role of Jefferson, several eminent students of his life and work have assured me that they can find no reference by him to the tragic end of his family in Kentucky, and one has even gone so far as to offer the opinion that Jefferson could not bring himself to discuss the appalling episode. If this is true, it is convenient for my poem, but the role of Jefferson in the poem does not stand or fall by this historical fact —which later research may prove not to be a fact at all. If the moral shock to Jefferson caused by the discovery of what his own blood was capable of should turn out to be somewhat short of what is here represented, subsequent events in the history of America, of which Jefferson is the spiritual father, might still do the job.

For the story of Meriwether Lewis, the first cousin of Lilburn and Isham Lewis, and a more distant cousin of Jefferson himself, whom he served as secretary for a time and to whom he stood in a sort of filial relation, we have the record, as kept by Lewis and Clark, of the great expedition to open the West and the biography of Lewis written by Jefferson after Lewis' death in Tennessee. There is some evidence, which does not strike me as completely convincing, that Lewis did not commit suicide, but was murdered, but Jefferson, in any case, believed that the death was a suicide committed in despair and resentment at the injustice of charges brought against his administration as Governor of the Louisiana Territory. My election of the theory of suicide is governed, however, by thematic and not by historical considerations.

I know that any discussion of the relation of this poem to its historical materials is, in one perspective, irrelevant to its value. I am trying to write a poem and not a history, and therefore have no compunction about tampering with facts. But poetry is more than fantasy and is committed to the obligation of trying to say something about the human condition. Therefore a poem dealing with history is no more at liberty to violate what the writer takes to be the spirit of his history than it is at liberty to violate what the writer takes to be the nature of the human heart. What he takes those things to be is, of course, his ultimate gamble.

This is another way of saying that I have tried to make my poem make, in a thematic way, historical sense along with whatever other kind of sense it may be happy enough to make. Historical sense and poetic sense should not, in the end, be contradictory, for if poetry is the little myth we make, history is the big myth we live, and in our living, constantly remake.

I wish to say a word about the form of this poem. It is in dia-logue spoken by characters, but it is not a play. The main body of the action is in the remote past—in the earthly past of the characters long dead—and now they meet at an unspeci-fied place and at an unspecified time to try to make sense of that action. We may take them to appear, and disappear, as their inner urgencies, and the urgencies of argument, swell and subside. The place of this meeting is, we may say, "no place," and the time is "any time." This is but a whimsical way of saying that the issue that the characters here discuss is, in my view at least, a human constant.

BROTHER TO DRAGONS

THE SPEAKERS *in the order of appearance*

THOMAS JEFFERSON: *The third President of the United States, who bought the Great West from Napoleon, but, in some ultimate vanity, neglected to mention that fact, or the fact that he had been President, when he composed the triple boast for his epitaph. The epitaph is now carved on his monument on the mountain where Monticello stands, in Albemarle County, Virginia:*

Author
Of The Declaration of
American Independence
Of
The Statute Of Virginia
For Religious Freedom, And
Father Of The University
Of Virginia

R. P. W.: *The writer of this poem*

DR. CHARLES LEWIS: *A physician, husband of Lucy Jefferson, the sister of the President*

LUCY JEFFERSON LEWIS: *Sister of Thomas Jefferson*

LILBURN LEWIS: *Son of Charles and Lucy Lewis*

LAETITIA LEWIS: *Wife to Lilburn Lewis*

AUNT CAT: *A slave in the household of Charles Lewis, and black Mammy to Lilburn*

BROTHER: *Of Laetitia Lewis*

ISHAM LEWIS: *Younger son of Charles and Lucy Lewis, and brother to Lilburn Lewis*

MERIWETHER LEWIS: *A cousin of Thomas Jefferson, and at one time secretary to him. With Clark, the commander of the expedition to open the Louisiana Territory and define the road to the Pacific. Upon his return, the Governor of the Territory*

GEORGE: *A slave*

PLACE: *No place*   TIME: *Any time*

JEFFERSON: My name is Thomas Jefferson. I am he
Whose body yet under the triple boast,
On my green mountain—

R. P. W.:   Yes, I've read your boast
Cut in the stone where your body still waits
On your green mountain, off in Virginia, awaiting,
I suppose, whatever fulfillment of the boast
May yet be.

JEFFERSON: The boast—it was the boast
That split my heart, the boast which I, in my late
Last year, made, while my heart still hugged some hope

That life had spoken and I'd heard it speak.

It was that boast that split my heart. It split it

As the vernal enlargement of life's green germ will split

The dry acorn. My heart, it was only my heart—

That old, earth-fallen acorn, dry, but postulating

Green germ and joy and the summer shade, and I had said:

Beneath that shade we'll shelter,

Green grandeur and unmurmuring instancy of leaf,

Through the heat of all the human day.

But I digress. If the boast did split my heart,

It was not in pain. But in pride. No, not pride—

That flame in the personal darkness, sucking

Heart-fat, heart-hope, all, like grease from a grease-lamp.

No, not pride. Or if in pride, then a pride past pride,

In my identity with the definition of man.

In Philadelphia first it came, my heart

Shook, shamefast in glory, and I saw, I saw—

But I'll tell you quietly, in order, what I saw.

To Philadelphia we came, delegates by accident,

in essence men:

Marmosets in mantles, beasts in boots, parrots in pantaloons.

That is to say, men. Like other men.

No worse, no better. Only ourselves, in the end.

Only ourselves, and what we then happened to be—

Offal of history, tangents of our fathers' pitiful lust
At midnight heat or dawn-bed ease.
Why should our fathers' long-lost lust
Seem pitiful? The twitch and gasp that was
The fuddling glory of our begetting seem
So pitiful? Is it not worthy of us?
Or we of it?—Too much crowds in
To break the thread of discourse and make me forget
That irony is always, and only, a trick of light on
                                  the late landscape.

But what I had meant to say, we were only ourselves,
Packed with our own lusts and languors, lost,
Each man lost, in some blind lobby, hall, enclave,
Crank cul-de-sac, couloir, or corridor of Time.
Of Time. Or self: and in that dark no thread,
Airy as breath by Ariadne's fingers forged.
No thread, and beyond some groped-at corner, hulked
In the blind dark, hock-deep in ordure, its beard
And shag foul-scabbed, and when the hoof heaves—
Listen!—the foulness sucks like mire.

The beast waits. He is the infamy of Crete.
He is the midnight's enormity. He is
Our brother, our darling brother. And Pasiphaë—
Pasiphaë, huddled and hutched in the cow's hide,

Laced, latched, thonged up, and humped for joy,
What was the silence then before the stroke?
And then your scream.
And through the pain then, like a curtain rent,
In your mind you saw some meadow green, or some grove,
Some childhood haven, water and birdsong, and you a child.
The bull plunged. You screamed like a girl, and strove.
But the infatuate machine of your invention held.
Later, they lifted you out and wiped your lips in

the dark palace.
We have not loved you less, poor Pasiphaë.

But no—I tell you, my mother's name was Jane,

Jane Randolph,
And she was born in the Parish of Shadwell, London.

I had not meant to speak thus. Language betrays.
What I mean is, words are always the truth, and always the lie,
For what I say of Philadelphia *now*
Is true, but true now only, not true *then*.
But this much then: We knew we were only men
Caught in our errors and interests. But I, a man,
Suddenly saw in every face, face after face,
The bleared, the puffed, the lank, the lean, all,
On all saw the brightness blaze, and I knew my own days,
Times, hopes, books, horsemanship, the praise of peers,
Delight, desire, and even my love, but straw

Fit for the flame, and in that fierce combustion I—
Why, I was dead, I was nothing, nothing but joy,
And my heart cried out, "Oh, this is Man!"

And thus my minotaur. There at the blind
Blank labyrinthine turn of my personal time,
I met the beast. And the time I met it was—
At least, it seems so now—that first moment
When the alacrity of blood stumbles and all natural joy
Sees Nature but as mirror for its fear,
And therefore, to be joy, must deny Nature
And leap beyond man's natural bourne and constriction
To find some justification for the natural.
Yes, then I met the beast. Well, better, indeed,
Had it been the manifest beast and the circumstantial
Avatar of destruction. But no beast then: the towering
Definition, angelic, arrogant, abstract,
Greaved in glory, thewed with light, the bright
Brow tall as dawn. I could not see the eyes.

So seized the pen, and in the upper room,
With the excited consciousness that I was somehow
Purged, rectified, and annealed, and my past annulled
And fate confirmed, wrote. And the bell struck
Far off in darkness, and the watch called out.
Time came, we signed the document, went home.
Slept, and I woke to the new self, and new doom.

I had not seen the eyes of that bright apparition.
I had been blind with light. That was my doom.
I did not know its eyes were blind.

Therefore all followed: the fat was in the fire.
Therefore all followed: and I who once had said
All liberty is bought with blood, now must say
All truth is bought with blood, and the blood is ours
Or we shall have no truth, and only the truth can make us free,
And doom is always domestic, it purrs like a cat,
And the only traitor lurks in some sweet corner of the blood.
Therefore I walk and wake, and I cannot die.
But I will tell you the story, how slowly, slowly the terror
                                                    drew on.
There was a house—

   R. P. W.: There was a house, and I have seen it, or saw,
Rather, all that remained when time and fire
Had long since done their kindness, and the crime
Could nestle, nuzzle, smug and snug, in any
Comfortable conscience, such as mine,
Or yours, and over the black stones the rain
Falls, falls with the benign indifferency
Of the historical imagination, and the grass
In idiot-innocence has fingered all to peace.
Well, anyway, I saw the house—

JEFFERSON: I never saw it. As you know, I never crossed
The mountains to Kentucky, and the West.
But I had sent good Meriwether there,
Across the plains and the last mountains, to the ocean,
To name and chart, and set the human foot.
But it was my West, the West I bought and gave and never
Saw, or but like the Israelite,
From some high pass or crazy crag of mind, saw—
I saw all,
Swale and savannah and the tulip-tree
Immortally blossoming to May,
Hawthorn and haw,
Valleys extended and prairies idle and the land's
Long westward languor lifting toward the flaming escarp-
                              ment at the end of day.
Saw the sad bison lick the outstretched hand,
And on the western rock, wracked in the clang and smother,
The black seal barks, and loves us, knowing we will come.
For wind is steady, and the moon rides gold,
Suns execute their arrogant processional
Of deep delight, and the illimitable glitter
Of distance dazzles to our human fulfillment.
It was great Canaan's grander counterfeit.
Bold Louisiana,
It was the landfall of my soul.
Or then it seemed—

R. P. W.:   But—

JEFFERSON: —there was the house.

CHARLES: I built it, and I know that some, perhaps you too,
Take it and all that came to pass therein
As mark of the hid madness and black spleen
I took from my father, and in my turn
Stuck in the womb of Lucy Jefferson
That she might conceive—and the child's first cry
Was honey in my heart, how long ago!

But if I was mad, and was vessel, vase, and propagator
Of madness, I'll tell you my madness' name,
And how I built the house. But I'll say, too,
Madness is but the cancer of truth, the arrogance
Of truth gone wild and swollen in the blood.

I built the house, left Albemarle and ease,
Took wife and sons, slaves, chattels, beasts, and goods,
Potions and pills, picked-lint, and scalpel, all
My marks of rank and occupation, all
Those things, intangible and tangible, that men
Clutch round them like a cloak against the time
The wind will shift, and sit sudden in the dire
Airt, and the cold creep.
I took those things, for they are like

The shell the shellfish spins from the slick slime
And deliquescence of itself to fend
That self, and its poor palpitation, boxed in dark.
Shellfish or man, the same. I, too. I took
Myself and mine,
Mine being myself,
And I fled.
Fled, that's the word. I fled the intolerable
World that I had made and that had made me.
It was intolerable only because
There was nothing intolerable in it: that world and I,
Two mirrors set forever and precisely face to face
To match but gaze for deeper gaze, and thus compound
The crime forever inward, each to each,
Of corridors infinitely empty, footless, shadeless, in one bright
And mutual smile of self-congratulation on success.

And so I fled,
Sought the new world, tension and test, perhaps terror.
Said I'd renew, if for an instant only,
The dear illusion, lost in youth, of being
Some part of human effort and man's hope.
Said I'd redeem the wild land, set blossom by the stone.
But knew it was illusion, and knew that I
Fled, not as redeemer but the damned, and damned
Because I had told the only lie man may
Not tell and live—at least, not tell himself,

And live:
The lie that justifies.

Ah, better, better, had I singly fled,
Alone and Ishmael where the desert howled
Or trees hid the savage's obscenity,
And better had hugged the foulness of uncivil men.
That had been honest, but instead I built
The house to house the lie I lived, and was,
And all the trophies of my emptiness.
But after the blood,
The blood and the midnight's awful utterance,
The flame took it.
It is gone.
And I am glad.

JEFFERSON: It is not gone, for I who never saw it,
See it, see it now, and in the incessant dark
Hear the timbers creak and the stair, untrodden, groan.
I have sometimes come to think in the late years
That the earth itself may groan for man's foot,
And be glad my foot is weightless now, but I know
That the impalpable is not the innocent,
For the house is gone and is not gone, and yet—

R. P. W.: I assure you it is gone. I know the place.
Up Highway 109 from Hopkinsville,

To Dawson Springs, then west on 62,
Across Kentucky at the narrow neck,
Two hours now, not more, for the road's fair.
We ripped the July dazzle on the slab—
July of '46—ripped through the sun-bit land:
Blunt hills eroded red, stunt-oak, scrag-plum,
The ruined coal-tipple and the blistered town,
And farther on, from the shade of a shack flung down
Amid the sage-grass by the blasted field,
A face fixed at us and the red eye glared
Without forgiveness, and will not forgive.
But touch the accelerator and quick you're gone
Beyond forgiveness, pity, hope, hate, love.
So we ripped on, but later when the road
Was empty, stopped just once to void the bladder,
And in that stunning silence after the tire's song
The July-fly screamed like a nerve gone wild,
Screamed like a dentist's drill, and then a million
Took up the job, and in that simultaneous outrage
The sunlight screamed, while urine spattered the parched soil.

Above Paducah, east some fifteen miles,
Upriver, there it is, they call it Smithland.
The town, I mean. It never came to much,
Sure not the vision and vainglory the man
Named Smith—whoever he may have been—had
In mind that morning when they laid the log,

Squared sill, mixed clay for chink, and split the shakes,
For the first cabin, back in the seventeen-nineties.
He had a right to hope, that fellow Smith,
In that heyday of hope and heart's extravagance
When Grab was watchword and earth spread her legs
Wide as she could, like any jolly trollop
Or bouncing girl back in the bushes after
The preaching or the husking bee, and said,
"Come git it, boy, hit's yourn, but git it deep."

And every dawn sang, "Glory, glory be!"
Sang, "Glory be to Grab, come git it, boy!"
Sang, "Git it, boy, hit's yourn, but git it deep!"

Smith had a right, all right; for the town-site
Was noble where the Cumberland discovers
The sober magnificence of the Ohio, and into that sweep pours
All its own wash and wastage up from Tennessee,
And the bluff was noble, and the beech it bore
To guard that stately confluence and observe
The traffic yawing westward, like a tide:
Broadhorn and keelboat and the boatman's hail
That shook the shallows while the fiddle skirled—
Half-horse, half-alligator, prodigal
Of blood, sweat, semen, and the God-damn world.
Haired hand on the sweep, and the haired lip lifts for song,

And the leathery heart foreknows the end and knows it will

not be long,

For a journey is only a journey and only Time is long;
And a river is only water, Time only will always flow
All the way from Shawneetown,
Long time ago.
That was the song the sweating boatman sang
While sunlight shivered and the green bluffs rang
All the way from Shawneetown, long time ago.

The last keel passes, it is drawing night.
The hickory leaf hangs limp, tomorrow weather.
Past spit and bluff-head now the last note fades
Into the reluctant opacities of history.
Past chute and snag, broadhorn and brawler gone.
They pass in music: *long time ago.*
They passed in music, and the river slept.
They passed in music; Smithland stays and sleeps.

Long time ago: and never came to much,
For Louisville up the river had the falls
And had the Blue Grass, too, to back it up.
Smithland had nothing, canebrake and gray clay,
And hoot owls aren't a poultry highly prized,
And even now no locomotive scares those owls.
A hundred years behind schedule right now,
Barring the Dixie Theater and gas pump,

It looks the sort of town Sam Clemens might
Grow up in now and not be much worse off.
River and catfish, nigger in the shade,
Little brick jail your fist could punch a hole in,
But the town bum's too comfortable to care,
It's good as home, or nigh, and his Baby Girl
Comes brings him hoecake like he likes it, hot,
And under the maples, from the courthouse pump,
Draws Pap fresh water. She is eight years old.

But this would not deny there's more in Smithland:
The pillow bitten in the midnight pain
Of love disprized or lust exacerbated,
Ambition burked and the ego oozing like
The secret sore and the suppuration smells,
Time's slow contraction on the most hopeful heart,
And all the moil and human jar, and every
Malice and stratagem and cankered dream.
For people live here, after all, and even
The picturesque bum, in the vomit-sodden dawn,
Cries out the classic anguish of our doom:
"Ain't nobody loves me, I never had no chance!"
And Baby Girl will hate him soon. Why not?

But if all this is true, the town is still
The sort of town that vagrant liar from Ithaca
Might describe as he once described his own rocky isle:
"Not much of a place—but good for raising boys."

Not rock and olive, sure, and the Ionian grandeur
Whence once Poseidon reared from his crystal courts
And corridors of glaucous pearl to stare,
Beyond black sea-wrack, whiteness of water, the brilliance,
In his majesty, foam-maned, upon the sun;
But a river will do when you are twelve. My own
Hometown, it didn't have that much, and wasn't,
God knows, a beauty spot, but there's no town
Without some country, and a ruined mill
And millpond, wood lot, and a fox's den
Can serve—or one wild goose that came one fall,
Lost from its own that like a constellation
Star-triumphing and steady thus bestrode
The imperial cold altitude, and the hoots died south.
Lost, sick, or old, it settled on a stock-pond,
And heard the arrogant clamor darkling fade,
And slept.
Kent shot it just at dawn, threw down his gun,
Crashed the skim-ice, and seized it, hugged it, ran
Three miles to town and yelled for joy and every
Step cried like a baby and did not know why.
Then at the barbershop the hangers-on
Admired the trophy, silent till one said:
"From Canady, come all that way, well I be durn."

Even without the goose you might have found
The images you'll need when you reach forty

And have to learn the single lesson left
To learn worth learning, and that lesson is
That the only thing worth learning you had learned
Long back before you laid the BB. down
For the .12-gauge. And that lesson is that the only
Thing in life is glory. That's a hard
Thing to learn, and a hard fact to face,
For it knocks society's values to a cocked hat,
Or seems to, for the one thing that man fears
Is the terror of salvation and the face
Of glory. But that face is all. Therefore,
Remember now your seeding and the world's magnificence,
To which the heart would answer if it could,
And sometimes can, and if it can't you'd better
Set your affairs in order and sit down
To the careful cultivation of cirrhosis,
For drink's a kind of glory too, and man
Can't live without some glory after all,
Even a poor kind.

And Smithland too,
Though it never came to much, had citizens
Who a century and a half were cramming their courthouse
With records of the things they lived by, if not for.
The records survive, debris of the local courts,
Circuit and County, in the fusty vault, blind:
Land transfers, grants, indictments, inquests, plaints,

Stompings and stabbings, public blasphemy,
Lawings and mayhem, and all the pitiful confusion of life,
Flung in a heap. And I thought of the kitchen-midden
Of a lost clan feasting while their single fire
Flared red and green with sea-salt, and the night fell—
Shellfish and artifact, blacked bone and shard,
Left on the sea-lapped shore, and the sea was Time.

Just out of Smithland on the Louisville road
You'll find the monument, a single shaft
The local D.A.R.'s put up in '24
Amid the ragweed and the cockleburr
To honor Lucy Lewis for her good taste
In dying in Kentucky. True, the stone
Does name her as sister to the President,
But quite neglects her chiefest fame, that she
Gave suck to two black-hearted murderers.
But let that pass, for to the pious mind
Our history's nothing if it's not refined.
But to return to Lucy, little's known—

LUCY: There is little to know, for I know only
The way the sunlight fell across a leaf in Albemarle.
So long ago in Albemarle. I know only
The tug of lip on nipple and how that small contraction
Made all my being hush to the deep depth
Like water windless under a moon of joy.

I loved my children. And love them. But know, too,
The way my husband's face looked locked in sleep,
When leaning in the night, the lamp unlit,
I said, "He lives in some dark place where I
May come to take his hand, if I love well."
But never came where he inhabited.
Came only to Kentucky, by my love.
I did the best I could. No, that's a lie.
I did not do my best. I died. I know
That if you love enough, and well, no death
Can come to kill you while there's need of you.
And there was need of me. Yes, if I had lived,
My love, somehow, might have sustained my son.
It might have been to him like a hand stretched out.
And for my other son, my love, somehow,
Might have been at least some light against the ignorant torpor
That breathed from the dark land. Yes, if I had loved,
Loved well enough to live, the tiptoe horror
Had not come sly and thus insinuated
Itself in my name to my dearest son.
This was my crime, who had forefeared the end,
Who whiffed the foul breath, caught the secret leer,
Forefeared and fled, who had seen all draw on.

I saw the dark land creep into my house.
I saw the dark night creep into my bed.
I saw the river-dark swim in my cup.

The screech owl laughed and told me I was dead,
And I believed him, and so I was dead,
And cannot die, nor cease to love and know
That the human curse is simply to love and sometimes to
love well,
But never well enough. It's simple as that.

R. P. W.: There's nothing of that on your monument,
But I know your name means light, and I'm sure
There was some need of light in that dark house.

LILBURN: They put it out! put out the light, they put
It out—and then, and then—

JEFFERSON: Look! that's the one,
The bloody brother and his hands, but look!
But look, his hands don't drip, his hands have nothing
On them, look, his hands—

LUCY: Oh Lilburn, oh, my son!

LILBURN: —and then, then it was dark. Listen, I'll tell you:
Do you remember when you lay and there was light,
But just one light, one candle flame, and all
The world was dark, and dark sniffed under the door?
Do you remember? Then the gust, the cold
Gust sudden, and the flame snapped, it snapped

Like a louse under the wind's thumb, and it was dark.
Or maybe just somebody came
And took the light away.

LUCY: Oh, son, my son! forgive me and let me die!

JEFFERSON: There's no forgiveness for our being human.
It is the inexpugnable error. It is,
Dear Sister, the one thing we have overlooked
In our outrageous dreams and cunningest contrivances.
And I who once contrived should know that now.
I know that now. Or do I? Do I yet?
For the old pain comes, the old nerve twitches whenever
Wind shifts, and fitful sits, if again for a moment,
In that sweet quarter of the heart where once
The breeze was steady, sun rose bright, and faith
Her fairest mansion held, and we were young.
Sister, we are betrayed, and always in the house!

R. P. W.: If you refer to the house Charles Lewis built,
There'll be no more betraying there unless
Spooks betray spooks; and in a spook house, too.
Nothing but rubble, and anyway to climb
That bluff would daunt the best conditioned spook.
I climbed it, and I know. It was July.
It's Lucy's monument that gives directions.
They're cut in stone of the obelisk's south face,

And tell you to ascend *the mountain which*
Can be seen in the distance one and one
Half miles to northward, up the Birdville Road.

The present owner's name is Boyle, Jack Boyle.
So the mailbox said, outside the whitewashed fence.
The house was white, a tidy bungalow.
The roof was tin, and blazing in the sun,
And zinnias blazed in the one flower bed.
A fat old collie panted in the shade.
I knocked and waited there for Mr. Boyle
To come and tell me I could climb the mountain.
"Sure can," he said, "if you ain't got good sense.
A day like this, and all that brush to fight."
That seemed ungracious, not in the country manners,
The only manners left that aren't for show.
But Mr. Boyle was just polite, no more,
And being polite that way, he hadn't reckoned
To name a man a fool on short acquaintance.
And so he grinned to disinfect the thing,
And said again, more heartily, "Sure can.
Sure can, but when you git up thar on top
Just one thing, please, just please don't go and bother
My rattlesnakes I'm fattenin up for fall."

Oh, he was quaint, or cute, was Mr. Boyle,
Or could be made to seem so.

But Boyle's not quaint because he speaks the tongue
His fathers spake, and holds his manners yet.
Or if he's quaint, he's quaint only as a man
Of moderate circumstances, modest hopes,
And decent ambitions, and he did his best,
Mortgage and weather taken to account
And minor irritations flesh is heir to.
Will do his best, no doubt, until he dies,
If he's not dead already, caught the flu,
Fallen off his tractor in the sun, or had
A coronary hit him on the street,
Down in Paducah, where he'd gone to trade.

Alive or dead, Jack Boyle has gone beyond me
And taken with him all the world he made—
Chiaroscuro and brilliance his expert eyeball painted
On all the intolerant emptiness of air,
Bold form and subtle involution his finger fashioned
In contact with the blind and groaning substance unde-
                           livered round him everywhere.
He's gone and a world's thus dead and gone beyond me,
And part of the world that's dead is I myself,
For I was his creation, too, that fleeting moment
I blocked his doorway and he stared at me,
A fellow of forty, a stranger, and a fool,
Red-headed, freckled, lean, a little stooped,
Who yearned to be understood, to make communication,

To touch the ironic immensity of afternoon with meaning,
To find and know my name and make it heard,
While the sun insanely screamed out all it knew,
Its one wild word:
Light, light, light!
And all identity tottered to that remorseless vibration.
I thanked him, turned away, got in my car,
And left myself dead on his porch, and he
Went into his house, to the shuttered cool, and left me
                                          dead, forever.

But after all, I had permission now
To climb the hill, and did so. Down the road
I parked the car in the best shade there was,
Got out, and left my father drowsing there.
For he was old, already pushing eighty.
No truth on mountains any more for him,
Nor marvel in the bush that burns and yet is not consumed,
Nor on the exposed height terror in the astonishing tonality
                                          of thunder.
For he had climbed his mountains long ago,
And met what face—ah, who can tell?
He will not, who has filled the tract of Time
With rectitude and natural sympathy,
Past hope, ambition, and despair's delectable anodyne.
What face he had met I do not know, but know
That in a café once, when an old friend said,

"Tell me about your father," my heart suddenly
Choked on my words, and in the remarkable quiet
Of my own inwardness and coil, light fell
Like one great ray that gilds the deepest glade,
And thus I saw his life a story told,
Its glory and reproach domesticated,
And for one moment felt that I had come
To that most happy and difficult conclusion:
To be reconciled to the father's own reconciliation.

It is most difficult because that reconciliation
Costs the acceptance of failure. And can we,
Sunk in our saeculum of desire,
Pay that cost?
Most difficult because that reconciliation
Signifies the purification of vanity.
And can we lift the hand,
Even to the most secret and worthy work,
If that hand be not sustained, and stained, in vanity?
Therefore most difficult because we know
The failures of our fathers are the failures we shall make,
Their triumphs the triumphs we shall never have.
But remembering our fathers, we are compelled to praise,
And for their virtues hate them while we praise,
And praising, wonder, caught in the sudden candid and
corrosive glare
Of speculation like the enemy rocket
Exploding above the torn and terror-bit terrain

Where darkness is the only comfort left—
We wonder, even as we consider their virtue:
What is wisdom and what the dimming of faculty?
What kindliness and what the guttering of desire?
What philosophic resignation and what the fatigue of the
                                        relaxed nerve?

But still, despite all naturalistic considerations,
Or in the end because of naturalistic considerations,
We must believe in virtue. There is no
Escape. No inland path around that rocky
And spume-nagged promontory. There is no
Escape: dead-fall on trail, noose on track, bear-trap
Under the carefully rearranged twigs. There is no
Escape, for virtue is
More dogged than Pinkerton, more scientific than the F.B.I.,
And that is why you wake sweating toward dawn.
More remorseless than the mortgage or glitter of the
                                        banker's *pince-nez,*
And that is why you wake sweating toward dawn.
More insidious than the cancer for which millions in re-
                                        search have not yet paid off,
And that is why you wake sweating toward dawn
And finger the cold spot in your side with no fantasy now
                                        for the matutinal erection.

For past all appetite and alibi,
And after your discourse and most honest deliberations,
                                        and after

The odor of fresh hay on the night wind
Like the perfume of a woman's parts, and past
Your various studies and most reasonable ambitions,
You know that virtue, like a syllogism,
Waits, has waited, and will wait, as on
The green leaf the lethal mantis at his prayer,
And under those great hands, spiked, Gothic, barbed,
Clasped high to arch the summer blue of heaven,
You pass, like an ant or aphid in the season's joy,
In browse or frolic, and that beast,
That green, crank nightmare of the dear green world,
All day, all day in sun and shade, maintains
His murderous devotion. He can wait.
Can wait, for you will come. For virtue is
Only the irremediable logic of all the anguish
Your cunning could invent or heart devise.

It was remembering my father that flushed these thoughts.
But now speculation settles like the dust
When wind stops, and there is only the great quiet of the
                                        sunlit space,
For I recall one Sunday afternoon,
How, after the chicken dinner and ice cream,
Amid the comics and word of the world's disaster,
I saw him sit and with grave patience teach
Some small last Latin to a little child,
My brother's child, aged five, and she would say

The crazy words, and laugh, they were so crazy.
There's worse, I guess, than in the end to offer
Your last bright keepsake, some fragment of the vase
That held your hopes, to offer it to a child.
And the child took the crazy toy, and laughed.
I wish you could tell me why I find this scene so sweet.

I left my father in the car to drowse
And went to climb the hill. I did it, too,
And just like Boyle had said, I was a fool,
A God-damned fool, and all that brush to fight.
Saw-vine and sassafras, love-vine, wild rose,
But the roses gone, and the tangled passion-vine,
And blackberry man-high and tangled like a dream,
And up the bluff, where cedar clambered rock,
The tall, hot gloom of oak and ironwood,
Canted and crazed but tall, and from their boughs
The great grapevine, a century old, hung in its jungle horror,
Swayed in its shagged and visceral delight,
Convolved from bough to bough, hawser and halyard,
Like rotten rigging of that foundered hill.
But I went on, and hit the carriage road
Old Lewis' Negroes had chopped from the live rock.
I hoped to God it wasn't in July
The black hands had grabbled and the black sweat dropped.
But niggers don't mind heat. At least, not much.
And sure, somebody's got to build the road.

Did I say road? Well, that's an overstatement.
You see the fallen buttressing, that's all,
Poor nigger stonework, and a century's gone,
And sluicing winter and the oak-root's heave
Have done their duty. And so I went on,
And damned the saw-briar, slapped the damned sweat-bee.
Went on, and all at once from the last green tangle, burst.
And there it was.

There was the quiet, high glade.
Blue grass set round with beeches, the quietest tree.
The air was suddenly sweet, a hint of cool,
And even the sun's blaze could abate its fervor,
And I stood in the new silence while my heart was beating.
Some cattle gazed like peace from the farther shade.
And there it was: the huddled stones of ruin,
Just the foundation and the tumbled chimneys,
To say the human had been here and gone,
And never would come back, though the bright stars
Shall weary not in their appointed watch
And the broad Ohio devotedly seek the sea.
I went up close to view the ruin, and then
It happened. Let me tell you how. You know,
When you have clambered hard and fought the brush
And breath comes short and both lungs full of cotton,
And your shirt is soaked and holds your hide like glue,
And heat runs prickling in your blood like ants—

Then if you stop, even in the blazing sun,
A chill will hit you and your bones will shake.

Well, standing there, I'd felt, I guess, the first
Faint tremor of that natural chill, but then
In some black aperture among the stones
I saw the eyes, their glitter in that dark,
And suddenly the head thrust forth, and the fat, black
Body molten flowed, as though those stones
Bled forth earth's inner darkness to the day,
As though the bung had broke on that intolerable inwardness,
And now divulged, thus focused and compacted,
What haunts beneath earth's primal, soldered sill,
And in its slow and merciless ease, sleepless, lolls
Below that threshold where the prime waters sleep.
Thus it flowed forth, and the scaled belly of abomination
Rustled on stone, rose, rose up
And reared in regal indolence and swag.
I saw it rise, saw the soiled white of the belly bulge,
And in that muscular distension I saw the black side scales
Show their faint flange and tracery of white.
And so it rose and climbed the paralyzed light.
On those heaped stones it was taller than I, taller
Than any man, and the swollen head hung
Haloed and high in light; then in that splendid
Nimb the hog-snout parted, and with girlish
Fastidiousness the faint tongue flicked to finick in the sun.

That fastidiousness was, I suppose, the ictus of horror,
And my natural tremor of fatigue converted to the
                                    metaphysical chill
And my soul sat in my hand and could not move.

But after all, the manifestation was only natural,
Not Apophis that Egypt feared and the redemptive
God Rē at each dawn slew, but could not slay,
Nor that Nidhogg whose cumbrous coils and cold dung chill
The root of the world's tree, nor even
Eve's interlocutor by Eden's bough.
No, none of these, nor more modestly in Kentucky
The quintessential evil of that ruin,
Nor spirit of the nigger boy named George
Whose anguish spangled midnight once like stars,
Nor symbol of that black lust all men fear and long for
Rising from earth to shake the summer sky.
No, none of these, no spirit, symbol, god,
Or Freudian principle, but just a snake,
Black Snake, Black Pilot Snake, the Mountain Blacksnake,
Hog-snout or Chicken Snake, but in the books
Elaphe obsoleta obsoleta,
And not to be confused with the Black Racer,
Coluber constrictor—oh, I remember
That much from the old times when like any boy
I thought to name the world and hug it tight,
And snake and hawk and fox and ant and day and night

All moved in a stately pavane of great joy
And naked danced before the untouchable **Ark of Covenant,**
Like Israel's king, and never one fell down.
But when you're not a boy you learn one thing:
You settle for what you get. You find that out.
But if that's all you settle for, you're good as **dead.**

But to return: old *obsoleta's* big,
Eight feet sometimes, and this was big, and he **reared**
Up high, and scared me, for a fact. But then
The bloat head sagged an inch, the tongue **withdrew,**
And on the top of that strong stalk the head
Wagged slow, benevolent and sad and sage,
As though it understood our human pitifulness
And forgave all, and asked forgiveness, **too.**
And that was all. With no haste, it was gone.
This really happened, the big black son-of-a-**bitch**
Reared from the stones, and scared me, for a fact.
There's no harm in them, though. And they kill **rats.**

JEFFERSON: Yes, they kill rats. I was a farmer **once,**
And know. And was a man once too, and know
That all earth's monsters are but innocent,
But one, that master-monster—ah, but once
I did not think so, for I thought him innocent, **too,**
And thought him—

R. P. W.:   Innocent?

JEFFERSON: I'm not a fool.

I saw the conduct of life. I saw the things
Men do, broadcloth and buckskin, friend and foe,
And the stench of action is not always sweetened
By the civet of motive, nor motive by good action.
For late at night by the infirm flame I had sat,
While wind walked over Albemarle and the oak groaned,
And sleet hissed on the pane, and blood winked
Low in the heart, and I kept my eyes only by
Effort of will on some disastrous page.
I read the books, and know that all night long
History drips in the dark, and if you should fumble
Your way into that farther room where no
Light is, the floor would be slick to your foot.

R. P. W.: But you said you once thought man—

JEFFERSON: Innocent?

Oh, yes, but even then I was no fool,
And knew that if you open the door of the cupboard
There are wood-violet and shanker, merd and magnolia,
                                        side by side.
And if I thought the housekeeping of Great Nature
Was wasteless and took all to beneficent use,
And decomposition and recomposition are but twin
                              syllables on the same sweet tongue
And two vibrations of the same string stung to joy,

I scarcely held that meditation on the nurture of roses
Is much comfort to a man who had just stepped in dung,
And philosophy has never raised a crop of hair
Where the scalping knife has once done the scythe-work.
For I was born in the shadow of the great forest,
And though the slave's black hand bore me, an infant, forth
From out that shadow, soft on the silken cushion,
From Shadwell out to Tuckahoe, I always
Carried the shadow of the forest, and therefore thought
That Man must redeem Nature, after all,
And if I held Man innocent, I yet knew
Not all men innocent, of darkened mind,
Ape's tickle and hog's slobber, and the shadow
Of the old trees, for he whom I sent forth
To redeem the wild world far to the Western Shore,
My near-son Meriwether, wrote in his papers
How the savage man wallowed in the horror of the *hogan,*
And lust was communal ceremony in the murk-filled lodge,
And such the reek of sour bodies and the contortion and
                                        pathos of the bestial face
That nausea was in your gut even as, for sympathy, your
                                        parts twitched.

And I have traveled in fair France, in that land
Of sunlight and the sunlit spirit that once
Itself shed light on all our faces and whatever face
Susceptive lifted to that genial ray,

But there—even there—I saw the abominable relics
Of carved stone mountain-high heaved up by what
Bad energy in what bad time, as though
Chaos had spewed her vomit up in stone
And frozen bubbles of disaster and contorted and crazed
Cairns of archetypal confusion, and from every
Porch, pillar, and portal stared
Beaked visage of unwordable evil or the snout
Of rapine, and fat serpents fanged themselves
To the genitals of women, whose stone eyes bulged out
As to distribute sightlessness on all, and the hacked mouth
Gave no scream you could hear across the long time, and
Vile parodies and mock-shows of the human
That might be beasts but yet were men,
Ass-eared, hog-hocked, and buzzard-beaked, and yet
With the human face of slack and idiotic malediction,
Stood about,
And approved all,
Approved
The sway of the world and knew, and were, our doom.
I'll tell you a secret—I've met them in the street.
I'll tell you another secret—it is a breed
That does not decrease in number or in exercise
Of significant influence in your own time.

But then, bemused by my conception of man,
I did not encounter such marvels in the street,
Or encountered without recognition. I encountered them only

As a depraved ingenuity in stone,
And took their congregation of shamefulness but to be
Shade of the Gothic night, and the old lubricity,
And but to be
Flotsam and the frozen foam
Of an ebbed disturbance in Time's tide,
The nightmare of a sick child who screamed in the dark,
And screamed that you must come to him,
But no one came, and there was the comfort only
Of some poor awkward Christ to foot the basilisk
(At Amiens, I think, he is), and the frail
Hope that all the monsters of man's begetting may be
Trodden by angels, triumphed on by saints.
But still he screamed, and screamed in the dark.
But then to Nîmes I came, and that Square House—

R. P. W.: I've been to Nîmes—long back, how many years?
I've been to Nîmes. There's good wine there, black,
Black as ink—you know, for you once had it there.
Three sous the bottle, you said you paid for it.
It costs a lot more now, but worth it still.
I drank the wine, slept in a decent bed,
And the next morning stood in the sun-gilt *place.*
I stood and stared at your "Maison Quarrée."

JEFFERSON: I stood in the *place,* and saw it. There is no way
For words to put that authoritative reserve and glorious
frugality.

I stood there, and I saw the law of Rome and the eternal
Light of just proportion and the heart's harmony,
And I said: "Here is a shape that shines, and here is
A rooftree so wrought and innocent of imprecision
That a man who hoped to be a man, and be free,
Might enter in, and all his mind would glow
Like a coal under the breath, in that precinct
Where the correctness of our human aspiration
Has body and abides and bespeaks the charmed space.

R. P. W.: So you—so you find evidence for innocence
In such a heap of organized rubble
(I call it cold and too obviously mathematical)
Thrown up by a parcel of those square-jawed looters
From the peninsula, stuck in a foreign land?

JEFFERSON: I think I know what the Romans were, and know
Better, perhaps, than you, and later when
A goat let drop his precise pellets, small and black on the
imperial mosaic,
And bats clustered, like raisins, in the split vault
Of the *thermae* of some pot-bellied World-Shaker,
Then Rome paid for what Rome was, and—

R. P. W.: Then what of the innocence you find?

JEFFERSON: I referred, my friend, to a time when I once
did find it,

And the Square House spoke to my heart of some fair time
Beyond the Roman tax-squeeze, and the imperial
Licentiousness, and the Gothic dark. It spoke
Of a fair time yet to come, but soon
If we might take man's hand, strike shackle, lead him forth
From his own monstrous nightmare—then his natural

innocence

Would dance like sunlight over the delighted landscape.
And he would need no saint or angel then
To tread the monsters, for man's own free foot
Would tread them down like vintage in the press,
And laughter, more extravagant than the Burgundian,

would racket

Round all the bright pendentives, coigns, and cornices of

the sky.

Ah, that—

R. P. W.: That?

JEFFERSON: That was only the old notion that propped

my heart and thewed up

My human arm. But that was then, not now.
For now all has been made clear to me, and I know now
It is the monsters slain that are innocent—the Hydra,
All hippogrifs and dragons, Grendel and Grendel's dam,
Are innocent. And as for the heroes, every one,
The Hercules of hairy thigh, and that David

Who danced his epicene minuet to the tune
Of the sling's twang, and the Cappadocian pig-sticker,
And that square-headed braggart of Hereot, high as the
mead-hall,
And Jack of the Beanstalk, too—yes, every one,
The saints and angels, too, who tread, yes, every
And single one, but plays the sad child's play
And old charade where man puts down the bad and then
feels good.
It is the sadistic farce by which the world is cleansed.
And is not cleansed, for in the deep
Hovel of the heart that Thing lies
That will never unkennel himself to the contemptible steel,
Nor needs to venture forth ever, for all sustenance
Comes in to him, the world comes in, and is his,
And supine yearns for the defilement of his slavering fang.
And I know this is true, and I will tell you.
And I have looked in the heart, and I will tell you.
There was the house, and I will tell you—

R. P. W.: Yes, I have read the records. I once intended
To make a ballad of them, long ago.
And I remember how the thing began:
> *The two brothers sat by the sagging fire.*
> *Lilburn and Isham sat by the fire,*
> *For it was lonesome weather.*
> *"Isham," said Lilburn, "shove the jug nigher,*

For it is lonesome weather.
It is lonesome weather in Kentucky,
For Mammy's dead and the log burns low
And the wind is raw and it's coming snow
And the woods lean close and Virginia's far
And the night is dark and never a star . . ."

Yes, it began about like that, but the form
Was not adequate: the facile imitation
Of a folk simplicity would never serve,
For the beauty of such simplicity is only
That the action is always and perfectly self-contained,
And is an image that comes as its own perfect explanation
In shock or sweetness to the innocent heart.

But first, our hearts are scarcely innocent,
And any pleasure we take in the folk simplicity
Is a pleasure of snobbish superiority or neurotic yearning.
And second, the action here is not explained
By anything in the action. It is explained,
If explainable at all, by our most murderous
Complicities, and our sad virtue, too.

No, the action is not self-contained, but contains
Us too, and is contained by us, and is
Only an image of the issue of our most distressful

self-definition.

And so to put the story in a ballad

Would be like shoveling a peck of red-hot coals
In a croker sack to tote them down the road
To start the fire in a neighbor's fireplace.
You won't get far with them, even if you run—
No, the form was not adequate to the material.

JEFFERSON: It never is. There is no form to hold
Reality and its insufferable intransigence.
I know. I know, for I once tried to contrive
A form I thought fit to hold the purity of man's hope.
But I did not understand the nature of things.
So I but dumped hot coals in that croker sack.
The fire burns through, the blood bleeds through, the bowels,
And not of compassion, are pierced, and foulness
Flows forth upon—no, I'll revert to the former metaphor:
If then I had known what I now know
I had thought it exquisitely better,
Given the courage, which perhaps I lacked,
To seize the hot coals of the human definition
In my bare hands, and scream, and run what steps
I could before I fell, and the white articulation
Of hand-bone trellised through the fire-black flesh.

R. P. W.: It was the white bone through the black flesh,
Fire-black and nigger-black, that got the brothers
Into their fix. White bone, and a dog that gnawed it.
We do not know what dog, what kind of dog—

Some frontier cur slinking the edge of forest,
Or some great brute bred up for bear and big
As a bear, or even one of Lilburn's hounds,
That Nero from Virginia he named in his will,
That is, in the codicil he scribbled the last day
Before he cried aloud and clawed the sod
On his mother's grave.

              We have to invent our dog.
Then make it Lilburn's hound that in effect
Will set the hot lead in the belly of the master
Who'd thought to name the loved animal in even
His one last hour, and will it to his father,
Across the mountains, in Virginia, oh, so far.
So make it Lilburn's hound, for irony.

We see it, liver-spotted, velvet-eared,
With gaze so wise and sad in faithfulness,
Crouched by the trace, on the new grass of spring—
The month is March—and for a background the incredible
Complication and arabesque of tender tendril,
Leafage, and bud, dappled in gold, and that heartbreaking
New delicacy of green—oh, sweet as hope—
That frets and freaks with joy this dark margin
And massive dark of forest. The forest reaches
A thousand miles in darkness beyond the frail human project.
But here the trace, the human track, and the hound

Crouching with head held high in a hint of heraldic
And leonine nobility, and under
Forepaws the human bone licked clean, or nearly,
Only some shred of fire-black flesh yet clinging.
What bone? Some bone the passer-by could see
As human and pick up and take to town.
Tradition says the jawbone of poor George.
Well, put the jawbone of poor George beneath
The forepaws of that hound, the faithful traitor,
It was the hound that—

JEFFERSON: The symbolism
Comes most sardonically apt. It was the hound
That Lilburn loved, the only thing alive
He loved, his mother—and my sister—dead.

R. P. W.: Do you really think he loved her? I should say
That his black need of her needs some other word.
Black need and justification for—

JEFFERSON: Love!
I apologize for introducing that word
Unthinking in some automatic and old-fashioned way.
No, I'm now ironical at your expense,
Or try to be—which is a way of saying—
Of saying what? Of saying what I cannot say,
Or bear to say. Well, God help me, I'll say it:

I have long since come to the firm and considered conclusion
That love, all love, all kinds, descriptions, and shapes,
Is but a mask to hide the brute face of fact,
And that fact is the immitigable ferocity of self,
And once you find it in your blood, and find even
That the face of love beneath your face at the first
Budding of the definitive delight—
That every face, even that one, is but a mirror
For your own ferocity, a mirror blurred
And breathed upon and slicked and slimed with love,
And through the interstices and gouts of that
Hypocritical moisture, the cold eyes spy out
From the mirror's cold heart, and thus self spies on self
In that unsummerable arctic of the human alienation.
And as I said, once you have learned that fact—

   R. P. W.: A little back you said you'd used the word *love*
In some unthinking and old-fashioned sense.
Well, I find your present definition
Just as old-fashioned, just as old-fashioned, say,
As Thomas Hobbes and his quaint nastiness.
And begging your pardon, this but goes to say
You lack a certain pragmatic perspective.

   JEFFERSON: What I lack, my friend, is the absolute dream
                              and joy
That I once had, and that from the way you talk
I doubt you ever had, for you—

R. P. W.: All right.
You're right, I never had it, for it is scarcely
The most fashionable delusion of my age, and I—
I simply never had it.

JEFFERSON: Well, I did.
I did, and that was joy until that fiend—

R. P. W.: You mean poor Lilburn?

JEFFERSON: Yes.

R. P. W.: There had been other
And equal fiends, and you, not being a child,
Had known the acts of evil.

JEFFERSON: Not in my blood,
For he was my blood. Listen—it is always
The dearest that betrays—

R. P. W.: Oh, yes, the hound!
Symbolically apt, you had said.

JEFFERSON: Yes, apt, because
We must always be betrayed by the most dear,
By what has taken food at our hands, and offered
Its silken self to our fingers, and laid its head

In some sweet crook of the arm, or heart. Well,
Such betrayal serves justice, for the beloved
Knows always the precise nature of our love,
Knows what it is, and therefore would be avenged,
Avenged for the least love-pat and the tutelage of fingers,
The imploring pinch in the dark hour and
The precise concourse of delicate tongue-tips and the
magnanimous

Act of forgiveness—yes, most for that, for that
Act is an index equal of desire
Gone craven with placation,
And of the self's final ferocity
Whetted in sweetness as a blade in oil.
Yes, forgiveness is the one unforgivable
Act, and—

R. P. W.: And so Lilburn forgave his wife.

JEFFERSON: Oh, yes,
That he might blame her too, in his act of forgiveness.

R. P. W.: Precisely. In that codicil they found
Beside the body on his mother's grave
He says: "And to that fair but cruel Laetitia,
Whose coldness unto me has brought on all"—
Or something about like that. I've seen the will.
But long before that blameful forgiveness, Laetitia

Lay invalid upstairs in the dark house,
Lay there at night and must have strained to catch
In the dark the drunken disputation below,
Where Isham and Lilburn huddled by their jug,
Summer and winter, and the attentive forest
Woke in the dark, breathed, and no leaf stirred.
Night after night thus, until that night
The scream came. Came once. Came twice. And came
Again, and filled the vault of the December dark, and—

LAETITIA: Yes, yes, that's right, it just filled up the room,
And the dark outside the room, and the whole world,
Or seemed to. Yet it wasn't loud, far off,
Being so far off, down there in the meat-house.
But soon as I heard it, it was like the world
Just started screaming by itself, and like I
Had just been waiting years for it to start,
And all my life had been waiting for it, and every
Dead leaf in the woods just screamed just like a tongue,
A little tongue, not loud, and maybe you couldn't
Hear one alone, it was so weak, but together
All screaming they made a big scream filling
Up all the world, and filled my head, and my poor head
Was one big hollow echo full of dark,
Big as the world, and the whole world, all the mountains,
The rivers, creeks, and fields and hills and woods and every
Leaf screaming in the dark, and all the stars,

Was in my head and lost, and my poor head
Kept whirling bigger. And I tried to scream.

But sometimes you can't scream, and I kept hearing
Somehow a voice that said, "Now! now!"
And kept on saying, "Now!" Like the time had come
You were afraid for, yet you had to have.
And even while I tried to scream I knew
I'd heard that voice before, just once before,
The first time ever Lilburn came on me,
And never a man e'er came on me before,
And it was Lilburn that I dreamed about,
But it wasn't a dream, and it was terrible
There in the dark like I was going to die,
And a voice in the dark said: "Now!"

                          Yes, I loved Lilburn
But everything was mixed, like my days and time
Had come to this, and I wanted to scream. But didn't.
And now was like that time, but worse. Oh, worse!
And the next I knew I was out on the stairs, and knew
I was going to fall. And suddenly I was happy,
Just knowing I was falling, and to fall
Might end whatever there'd been to scream about
For all those years, and now, but I couldn't scream.
And so I fell.

R. P. W.:   But next day got away.
Yes, that's the mystery, how you got away.
No word in the record, and you an invalid,
Or sort of one at least. And it's sure Lilburn
Wouldn't let you leave, to go and start the talk.
Yes, Laetitia, how did you manage it?

LAETITIA: You know how colored folks are, just like children.
Be nice to them, and they'll be nice to you,
And I was lonesome in that big old house,
And big old bed, and talked to old Aunt Cat
For lonesomeness. She was a good old thing,
And she'd been Lilburn's nigger Mammy, too,
And gave him tiddy like he was her own
And loved him good, and loved him still, her Chile.
And when my spells came bad, she did what she could,
Put vinegar on my forehead and rubbed my wrists.
It was Aunt Cat who made me get away.

Next morning when I woke I was abed
Where Lil had put me—he'd found me on the stairs—
And Aunt Cat by the bed when my eyes first opened.
And so I said, "God, God, oh, God," not loud,
Or thought I said it, just to see the room
Yet like it was, and nothing changed, and to know
The whole world like it was, and nothing changed.
I couldn't recollect what had happened, only

I knew something had happened and was terrible.
So I said, "God, I just can't stand it, God."
But didn't know what it was I couldn't stand.

And then Aunt Cat leaned close, and I could see
The red lines in her old yellow eyeballs,
And her breath was old and came out over the yellow
Old broken teeth, and just that single second
I didn't know her, who she was, and the face
Was awful, and the breath came out. The breath,
It said: "I'll git a hoss." And I said: "What?"
And the face came close, and I was scared, and the breath
Said: "You go."

        I said: "I'm sick."

              And the face
Then said: "Hit's the Lawd's last chance, I heared the Lawd,
I heared Him say last night when the yearth shook,
I heared Him say, one shall be saved—"

                  And suddenly,
It looked like I could recollect something,
And I said: "Last night—did the earth shake—really shake?"
And she said: "Chimneys come down, and trees, and the water
Sloshed and roared in the river, and the Lawd said—"

R. P. W.: This was December 15, 1811,
That night, and that the night of the great earthquake,

When the Mississippi ran back north three days,
And the earth split wide and moaned like a cow with calf,
And Reelfoot Lake was made, and New Madrid
Fell down, and oak trees snapped like a blacksnake whip.
The disturbance lasted into February,
But that night was the worst.

CAT: Yeah, Lawd, the worse,
And the river sloshed and roared, and the Lawd said—

LAETITIA: And when Aunt Cat said that to me that day
The funniest thing happened, and I marveled slow.
I marveled slow to recollect, and I said:
"Then it wasn't just my head, it was the earth
Shook, too, and threw me down." She said: "The Lawd,
He give a sign." And the face was awful, and the breath
Came hot and rancid, and it said: "You go!"
And I heard my voice far off, and it said: "Yes."

It was just Aunt Cat, and she loved me, and she said:
"The hoss is saddled, I saddled him, you go,
Go now, afore they knows—and when they knows,
Ain't nothin they kin do but beat me—" Then,
Of a sudden, said, "Oh, Lawd, oh, Lawd, jest let 'em
Jest beat me, nothin else!" And I popped up
In that big old bed and saw her face, and I recollected,
And my breath came sharp, and I said: "Last night—last night
Somebody yelled, somebody yelled—"

                                But her eyes

Rolled once or twice, like nigger eyes will roll.
She looked round quick, said: "Hesh." And I said:
"But somebody yelled." And she said: "Hesh." Said: "Hesh,
Hit won't be me what tells it, and him my Chile."
And I said: "But somebody yelled." And she said: "Lawd!"
And wouldn't tell a word, but hesh, and me to ride.
She helped me get away, she loved me so much.

R. P. W.: She loved you so much, yes, that's one way to put it.
Or hated them, for that's another way
To put the reason, and there's nothing strange
In that, for every act is but a door
Between two rooms, on equal hinges hung
To open either way, on either room,
And every act is Janus-faced and double,
And every act to become an act must resolve
The essential polarity of possibility.
Thus though the act is life and without action
There is no life, yet action is a constant withering
Of possibility, and hence of life.
So by the act we live, and in action die.

No, that's not the thought I had meant to follow.
I had meant to say that if the act resolves
The essential polarity of possibility,
It yet will carry that polarity,

As deep in the inner flesh of autumn fruit
We trace the frail configuration of spring's flower.
But that image, with its sense of beauty and delight,
Is scarcely appropriate for my notion, and my own line
Has a sort of conventional euphony and sweetness.

All wrong: For the origin of no human action,
No matter how sweet the action and dear, is ever
Pure like the flower. For if sweetness is there, then bitter-

ness too,

In that hell-broth of paradox and internecine
Complex of motive and murderous intensity
We call the soul, and from that
Anguish of complication any act,
Any act at all, the bad, the good, affords,
Or seems to afford, the dear redemption of simplicity:
The dear redemption in the mere fact of achieved definition,
Be what that may.

Can man wish more than knowledge?
Did that poor fellow Lilburn long for more?
Or strive for other when the thunder-flare
Of midnight vision burst, and sudden, he saw
The world heave like the forest in a storm,
Heaving
In exultation of dishevelment
Beneath the blue blaze of the splitting sky,

While darkness danced on tiptoe far above
The last torn cloud and tore the streaming and apocalyptic
Horror of its enormous hair?

                    I refer
Not to the earthquake just a little after
The business in the meat-house had been most
Satisfactorily concluded. I refer,
Simply, to that electric and powerful moment
Of Lilburn's first awareness when he knew
At last, at last, the thrilling absoluteness
Of the pure act to come. Ah, he yearned toward
The peace of definition. Here it was.

So much for Lilburn, but it's now Aunt Cat
That we're concerned with—if for love or hate, or both,
She sent Laetitia out. She loved her, yes,
But, oh, she knew Laetitia was the sure
One instrument, one weapon, that she had.
So sent her to her brother, sick and gabbling,
Gabbling in terror with no word of fact,
But terror worse than fact, as Aunt Cat knew.
So sent her forth, so cocked the trap, dug the pit,
And fired the fox-tail for the Philistine wheat.
She knew the simple classic formula:
Divide the white folks and sit back and wait.
But Aunt Cat still loved Lilburn—yes, that's true

In the way such things are true. She'd given him suck,
And she was his black Mammy, so she now
Just wouldn't tell Laetitia, not a word,
Just "Hesh," and "Hesh." It wouldn't be her mouth
That told the tale, what happened in the meat-house.
So she was guiltless. Who could blame Aunt Cat
If Laetitia now in her dark, gabbling fear
Could work out all her hate of Lilburn?

LAETITIA: Stop!
I didn't hate him. And I love him still.
I guess I do. At least, when I remember
How I first saw him, all the feel comes back
And something in my middle goes all soft
And sort of sick, but it's a sick all sweet,
And my knees go funny like I'd just fall down.
Yes, right this minute now when I remember
The first time e'er I saw him. 'Twas Big Court Day,
And folks all came and filled the settlement,
Came into town and made a sight to see,
All kinds, and some the folks that cleared for corn,
And forest folks from where the dark woods are,
All lank and skinny and got leather shirts,
And tote their guns and ever walk so sly,
And Indians, too, but not a kind to scare you,
Just poor and dirty and they scratch themselves,
And swamper folks and men from off the river,

With red rags round their necks and eyes that stared
Like they would scare you, and black whiskers wild.
And folks was drinking likker and they sang,
Sang "Barby Allen," sang "Shoot the Buffalo,"
And yelled for fun and made their brags and laughed,
And some were fighting over in the shade.

Who 'twas, I never knew, but came a yell,
A different yell and not a yell for fun,
It made you shiver, it so sad and wild.
Just once, and then somebody came and told
How 'twas a fellow got his eyes gouged out,
The way folks thumb them out when they get fighting.
For mad or fun, it's just the way folks fight.
Who 'twas, they said he bragged and fought for fun.
Who 'twas they never named, but he was blind.
And I was marveling what a funny yell,
And tingly-wild and sweet to make you cry.
And sunshine came so pretty everywhere,
For it was spring now, and winter gone and departed.
And I—I felt like crying to see the sun so pretty.

Then I saw Lilburn, but not to know his name.
Across the crowd, just sitting on his mare.
And sat so easy, too, and limberlike,
Just sitting sideways while he leaned and talked,
His left hand on his hip and the right just laid

On the mare's curved neck, a-fiddling with her mane.
And when the mare got restless and she danced,
So limber Lilburn's waist just moved with her moving,
So sweet to see, but his shoulders never moved,
And his face was dark and beautiful and still.
And when she danced too much, his hand went strong,
Strong of a sudden on her neck, and she—
Why, she was quiet then underneath his hand.
And then—and then it happened and I shook.
And clear as day and sudden and so strong
I felt the hand on my own neck, and I was still.

I just stood there and looked across the crowd,
And thought that if that man whose very name
I didn't even know just moved his hand,
Even just one finger on his mare's round neck,
I'd just fall down and die, I was so happy.
The hand was strong on my neck, and the fingers hard.
And all the pretty sunshine was swimming with my tears.

But I didn't fall down, I just stood there and loved him,
And didn't know his name, and said right sly
To Sudie Persley standing there beside me—
We girls just stood together like was proper
And nice for girls come in to see the sight.
So I said: "Sudie, see that funny man,
The man on horseback there so swart and strange?

I said it that way just to fool her, for I
Just thought I'd die if she knew what I felt.
But she was sly and looked at me right sharp,
And laughed, and pinched my arm, and said: "Oh, silly,
You silly goose, you're flying awful high!
Don't you know who that is?" And I said: "No."
And she: "Why, silly, that is Lilburn Lewis,
He's Lilburn Lewis lives at Rocky Hill,
And, silly, aren't you flying awful high?
Why, he's the nephew of the President
And true-blood kin to old Tom Jefferson."

JEFFERSON: Yes, that's the fact that shakes my heart with
          the intrinsic shock:
Born of my sister's body, vessel of my blood,
And yet what it is. It was a parcel of flesh
That my sister's body ejected, squeezed out, dropped,
And they cut the cord and trammel of that parcel
But could not cut the cord that bound her heart
To that parcel of unformed flesh. They should have thrown it
Out where the hogs come to the holler, out with the swill.

No, it's my fault. I tell you what I should have done
When I first saw it and it lay on the lace pillow—
You know an infant's face, wizened and seamed
And of no beauty, yet when that sweet parcel of flesh
Is laid on the lace pillow, your heart stirs.

It stirs at a new sense of innocence and the human

possibility.

But I tell you, the wizened mark and seam are not the mark

Of some new possibility of innocence but are

Prefiguration of the face of vile age

When every seam is but a scar and notation

And the malign calligraphy of old indulgence,

Hatred, perfidy, slyness, rage, and such incidental

Desires as glut our time and mark us as men,

And truth pocks faces like a foul disease.

Look at my face. I could very easily tell you

What appetite's crookt heel here slewed and spurned

And passed, and passing, marked the flesh like disturbed mire,

But I am old, and being old, am the record of my failure,

And being old, need tell you nothing. All is clear.

And I am what I am, but whatever I am,

And whatever you make of my face, and failure,

I still reject, cast out, repudiate,

And squeeze from my blood the blood of Lilburn.

I affirm it is not of my—

LUCY: Brother! I beg you,
For the sake of your own soul and salvation—

JEFFERSON: That's why
I cast him out, to have at least a soul
If not salvation.

LUCY: Don't you remember him little?

JEFFERSON: Yes, and I'll say what I should have done then.
Listen, the Indian, when some poor frontier mother, a
captive, lags
By the trail to feed her brat, he'll snatch its heels
And snap the head against a tree trunk, like a whip.
Just so, and the head pops like an egg. Well,
There wasn't any tree, it being indoors, but the brickwork
Of the chimney in your room would have been perfectly
adequate.
And listen, dear Sister, now don't you wish I had done it?

LUCY: No. No. For there was the time he was little and lay
Sweet to my arms—

JEFFERSON: Well, I scarcely imagine
That George, the colored boy, would share your views.
Or for that matter, Laetitia when she fled,
Hung sick and shivering on the horse, and fled.

LAETITIA: I just hung on, hung on the best I could.
I made the settlement, and somebody there
Rode out to tell my brother, and he came,
And the world shook again that afternoon, and chimneys,
They tumbled down, and folks named the End of Time,
And the world shook and folks fell down to pray.
And I prayed too. But I just prayed for the end.

R. P. W.: And so you prayed, but it was not the end.
It takes something more to bring the End of Time
Than what came there that night in your meat-house.
For that, as a matter of fact, was no end and no beginning,
Just an episode in the long drift of the human
Narrative, and impressive chiefly for
Its senselessness. And there's always and forever
Enough of guilt to rise and coil like miasma
From the fat sump and cess of common consciousness
To make any particular hour seem most appropriate
For Gabriel's big tootle. For instance, the folks fell down
Right in the road and prayed, but couldn't have any idea
Of what had happened in the meat-house. It was other
Quite different things, and for each man a different
Set of peculiar and well-fondled reasons,
That made that hour seem perfectly made to order
For the world's end, as this present hour would seem
To any of us if the earth shook now and the sun darkened—
To any of us, that is, if we weren't so advanced
Beyond the superstitious fear of God's Wrath.

LAETITIA: I wasn't afraid of what the Lord might do.
I was afraid of what He might not do.
I was afraid He might not send the fire.
So I rolled my head on the pillow there, and prayed
For the End of Time, after all had happened to me.

R. P. W.: It's off the point, but what I can't understand
Is how something didn't happen quick to Lilburn.
Your brother finds you in a state, wild-sick,
Run off from Lilburn's house, yammering with fear—
Well, Old Kaintuck was not a community
Famous for indirect action. You had a brother,
And even if the Lewises were great—

BROTHER: Look here, there won't be any of that kind of talk.
No man e'er said I was afraid of him,
Or never said it but once. Just let a man
Do something to my sister he hadn't ought to,
And I'd know why, and they don't come too big.
You give me a reason—you know, to provoke a man—
And I'd step right up and pull Jesus Christ off the cross
And make Him talk turkey, even if folks did say
His Pappy was a big man in the home section.
Lewises, hell. A Lewis ain't got but two balls
And hung in the same place like anybody else.
And I never took much shine to Lilburn, no way.
Oh, he was polite and never uppity.
Just once a man gets uppity with me.
He named me "Brother" to him, sweet as pie,
And I'll say this, he was a man and stout
And not afraid of nothing, nor nobody,
And nobody in Livingston County thought it different,

But there was something 'bout him, hard to say.
There was just something, the way his face was—

LAETITIA: Oh, it was still but it was beautiful!

BROTHER: Well, that sounds sort of laying it on to me.
But there wasn't a thing wrong with the looks he had,
Except there was something wrong. Sometimes his eyes
Just stared at you so bright for just a minute.
Black eyes they were, but with a kind of shine,
And like he was looking through you—

LAETITIA: Oh, I know,
And how I felt. I felt I'd just fall down.
At least it was that way the first I knew him.
It was the Persley house where we first talked,
Before the big in-fare when Sudie wed.
And when the fiddles took up high and clear
To give the reel and make the folks all happy,
The music was all sparkly-bright like fire,
All spangly-bright, but sweet, and sweet like fire,
And music in the air but in me too,
And burning in me spangly in the dark,
And Lilburn took my hand and his eyes were shining.
His eyes just had that shine, and my breath was short.

BROTHER: He had a way to look at a man sort of

Like you weren't there, like you was just nobody,
And ain't no man gonna—

LAETITIA: Oh, I was nothing,
Just nothing when he looked, and I wanted to be
Just nothing and him everything, but me
A nothing that somehow was part of every
Sweet part of him, and sweet to be, like air,
Like air he breathed and didn't know or heed,
Or maybe water he was swimming in,
And splashed and lolled, and water's got no name,
But I'd just hold him up, and be round him everywhere.
Oh, that was then—

R. P. W.:   But then?

LAETITIA: Then it got different.
Just how it started I don't know. It wasn't
A thing it looked like I could know, it wasn't
A thing to lay a name to, and I reckon
There's just no name to lay to the worst things,
And that's what makes them worse than anything,
For if they had a name, then you could name it.
At least to name it would be something then,
If you could bear to name it. And I think—
I mean I've come to think—that I could bear now

To name most anything if I could know,
Just only know, the name to name it with,
Even the worst.

               But what's the worst? That's awful—
It's awful not to know what the worst is.
For if you don't know that, I reckon there's nothing,
Not anything, to know, and if you don't know
Not anything, then, God—oh, God—then all
My life and living was just nothing, God,
And I am nothing, God—and oh, dear God,
Not even if You're God and made the world,
And take a mind, with one big huff-and-puff,
Could blow the moon and stars across the sky,
Like a boy just blowing dandelion fuzz,
And leave the sky all dark, or take a mind,
Grab down the sun and squeeze it in your hand
And not get burned, and the sky all dark forever—

Oh, God, even if You're God, You haven't got
The right to make me not know anything
And make my life all nothing then, and me
Just nothing. And all I want, dear God, is a name
To name it with and not be nothing, God.
I don't ask much, just to know what it came to, God.

R. P. W.: You don't ask much. Yet you ask everything,
And maybe just the one thing God can't give.

Or anybody. Merely the last thing,
The thing you're stuck with, to figure out for yourself.
All you demand is definition, too,
Just like poor Lilburn. Do you hate him less
To think that he, like you—

LAETITIA: Oh, I don't hate him!

R. P. W.: As I was saying, do you hate him less
To think that he, like you, like you at the last,
Was only trying to know what the good thing was,

                                        and when

He couldn't know the good, then did the worst,
Whatever the worst thing was, he did to you?

LAETITIA: I tell you, I don't know what the worst thing was,
And whether he really did whatever it was
Or it just sort of happened to him, too,
Like it happened to me. Oh, he could be so sweet,
So sweet and gentle too. That is, sometimes,
Like once we rode by the woods and it was fall,
And sunshine e'er so bright and the trees bright-colored,
And one big sweet gum golder than the sun
With sunshine on it bright to make it golder.
And he rode up and stood high in his stirrups
To pull a piece and cut it with his knife,
And held it in his hand and looked at me.

You know how sweet gum is, the leaves like stars?
Like stars all gold, and he held them in his hand.
I watched him hold them, and I rode up slow.

Then, "Stop!" he said, and pushed my cape-hood back,
Then slow and careful, leaf by leaf, he put
The sweet-gum stars all round, stuck in my hair.
And said: "Your hair's all gold, Laetitia, gold, and now
The stars are in it gold. I put them there."
My hair's not gold, just sort of washy brown,
But I felt sweet to hear him name it gold,
And while my heart got big and glad, he looked,
And said: "Oh, you're an angel from the sky."
And he was smiling like I never saw.
But sudden, then—like puff, and the candle out—
His face was dark, and darker than the night.
He grabbed my wrist so hard, and leaned at me,
And said: "If you're an angel down to earth,
Then I simply give you one piece of advice:
Go!" And watched my face, and laughed right short,
And said: "Go back to Heaven if you can,
And if you can't, then try the Other Place,
For—" and flung my wrist down hard and said
"—I tell you, even Hell would be better than this sty."
The sun fell bright and gold on all the world,
But he rode on and never said a word.

And then night came, and I lay in the dark, alone,
With Lilburn gone and left me long before,
And didn't tarry for his supper even.
But middle of the night, I heard him come,
And knew he'd been down to the settlement
And drinking whisky at the tavern there.

That's where he used to take his brother Isham,
Young like he was and just a boy well grown,
And kind of sweet, and he just loved Big Bubber.
Whatever Lilburn did, why, he was God,
And Isham copied Lil, who was so stout.
They used to wrestle of an afternoon
To pass the time, for Isham pestered Lil to.
And once when Isham almost had him, Lilburn
Gave a loud laugh, and twisted like a cat,
So quick, and grabbed, and grabbed him sly and hard,
And flung him down, so hard you heard the crack.
Then stood and said: "You got to eat some more
Corn bread and buttermilk to be a man."

And Isham lay not moving. Then I saw
Big tears grow in his eyes, and grow and spill.
He lay on his back, and the tears just overflowed
So quiet, it was the quiet that scared me then.
I ran to him, but just when I leaned over,

Lil said: "Don't touch the bugger, let him lie."
Then said: "Cry-baby, cry." And spat. And walked away.

R. P. W.: So that's the worst, you say? Well, if—

LAETITIA: Oh, no!
It's something else. And different, too, and worse.
I reckon I just started telling this thing
So as not to think about the other, not
To even know it ever happened, just
To forget I've got to tell it soon and will feel
The words grow in me, and they hurt to come.

But you can't forget, not anything that happens,
For forgetting is just another kind of remembering.
No, that sounds silly. But it's not silly. It's true.
No, it's a kind of true, like crazy-true,
The way bad things can come to you and happen,
And you say: "Oh, no—this isn't me, not me,
Not bad like this to me—for I'm Laetitia,
I'm little Tishy—" and I played beside the river
And sang a song to make the river run,
And the river ran and sparkled, it was summer,
And birds sang, too, and I was nice and good,
And minded Mamma, and when the sun got low
She called to me, and I took my doll and went,

For it was night, or nigh to coming on.
They named me Tishy. I was little then.

Oh, you, you know now what I'm trying to say.
How you can't believe it's you things happen to,
And if they're true, they're only crazy-true,
Like forgetting being a kind of remembering,
Yes, crazy-true and awful, and I heard Lilburn.
He made a noise out there on the stairs, and I knew
How he'd come back from down there in the tavern,
Down in the settlement. For Mother Lewis,
That time she was alive, and Lilburn then
Just drank in the tavern when his blues came on.
And not at home. You see, he loved his mother.
He was good to her, always.

LUCY: Yes, always, to me.
And he loved me, and if there is love at all—
Oh, Laetitia,
If love at all, if just a grain, no matter,
No matter the kind or shape, oh, my dear Laetitia—
My dear, whatever it is, it is precious.
But I, I made the repudiation. I died.
I lay and knew the end, and then I saw
His face. But a wide world between, like a valley,
Like a wide valley, and the rain fell steady between,
So steady and gray and you hardly see beyond,

Where the far hill is, and far across the valley
So full of the rain falling, I saw his face.
It was big as the hill, but the hill was small with distance,
And distance was dim and the rain without ceasing.
The distance was but to the bed-foot, but a great
Distance, and a wide valley where the rain fell.
And so I could not clearly distinguish his face.
But knew it yearned toward me, and I cried, "Oh, God!"
At least, my heart uttered a cry: "Oh, God,
I will go back and endeavor anew
The blessedness of the human obligation."
But the valley was wide and the rain fell steady,
And then I could see nothing, but heard the sound of the rain.
And when in my dark the rain no longer contrived its
                                        consistent whisper,
I knew that I was dead. But cannot die.
And, oh, Laetitia—

LAETITIA: And he was on the stairs,
And coming in, in the dark, and I knew it would happen,
Whatever it was, and I knew in the dark, I just knew
Like you know at night in the wild woods, you don't hear
It breathe, or a paw move even, but you know—
I lay in the dark and heard him breathe and move.
And then he was there. And soft, so soft, he said:
"Laetitia." And I said, "Yes," and hearing his voice,
One second, for just one second, I forgot

That I knew it was going to happen, whatever it was,
For he said—and not yet in the dark had touched me—
For he said: "Do you love me, Laetitia?" And I said: "Yes."
In a voice so far and thin like somebody else.
Then he said, "Ah," in the dark, like a sigh. Said: "Ah."
Then he did it.

       And it was an awful thing
I didn't even know the name of, or heard tell—
Or if I had heard tell, I'd plain forgot,
It was so awful that folks could do so awful.
But when he did it, even if I'd never heard,
It came just like an awful remembering,
Like it had happened long back, not now, not now,
And I wanted to say, "Stop!" But I couldn't say a thing,
For if a thing is just an awful remembering
That comes from you deep inside, then you can't say, "Stop,"
For it's already happened, and deep inside, and it's you.
And besides, it was Lilburn, and you know I loved him.
No matter how awful that folks could do so awful.
And I—why, I—

BROTHER: Look here, if you just told me,
I'd stopped his clock, for ain't no man, nobody,
Going to do dirty to my sister, no matter
What kind of dirty and—

R. P. W.:   So that was the worst, Laetitia?

LAETITIA: The worst? Why, no—there was next day to come.
And if that wasn't the worst—but I don't know.
It was next day, toward sun, and we sat by the fire,
With night coming on and the gray light filling the land,
For it was clouds today, not like yesterday
When sunshine had made the sweet-gum tree all gold,
And we didn't talk, and I could see out the window,
Way down the bluff and over the flat land, way off.
The river was there and had a kind of gleam-like,
Not sun, for the sun was shady and night nigh,
But just like the river gave off some light and it cold,
Like a knife that lies in the shadow and the blade
Gives off a light with a gleam-like, so still and cold.
And grayness was slow over all the flat land,
And I tried not to think but be still like the land and the
                                                gray light.

But Lilburn said: "Do you love me, Laetitia?" He said it.
And what could I say? For I loved him, I loved him, no matter.
So I said: "Yes." And he pulled his chair up close,
And took my hand to kiss it, and kissed it. And said:
"My poor Laetitia, I love you." And what could I say?
For all things that ever had happened were only a dream,
And this the real, and the realness his mouth on my hand
And the firelight dancing so little and pretty in the dark room.

So I said: "Yes. I know." And then his head
Rose up, and he looked so steady till I was nothing,

Nothing but sweetness, and then he whispered low:
"Last night, remember?"

               And then my heart stopped.
It was like you stepped in the dark and nothing was there.
And it happened again in my head, and might happen
                            forever,
So I said: "Yes."

            And he said: "Ah." And said:
"Ah, Laetitia—now tell me exactly what happened."

But my words wouldn't come, and my poor chest was
                          a bigness
That hurt but was not words, and suddenly I said:
"I can't, I just can't tell you." He jerked away:
"Oh, you never loved me, you never loved me, not ever!"
And jerked his arms wide, like he wiped the world away.
And I—I just cried out: "Oh, Lilburn, I love you!"
But he stared at me, and said just one word: "Love."

And the word was like he spat it out from his mouth,
Like spit hawked up and cold on your tongue and you spat it,
And I saw the word on the floor right where he spat,
On the board like a glob to quiver and glimmer a gleam-like,
And the word just lay and quivered cold where he spat,
And it—why, it was love.

And that was awful,
To see the word there slimy and cold, the word
For what had been sweet in you. It was too awful.
So I cried out, before my heart would break:
"Oh, Lilburn, Lil, I'll say it!" And he said: "Ah."
And took my wrist to hurt, he was so strong,
And squatted by me there, and the fire fell low.
Said, "Ah," and leaned, and the last fire lit his face.
His face—his face was beautiful and still,
And the bigness that in my chest had hurt me so
And was not words, was words now, and they came,
And some were words I never named before,
They were so awful maybe, nor heard tell,
But there they were, and words for what had happened,
And was happening again in my head, and might now
Just go on happening forever, wake or sleep,

But I said the words, and my body seemed to float
So light and high. Then the words were over and done,
Like rain or wind had stopped, and now I'd sleep,
And sleep forever, no matter the things in my head,
For all that had happened that night before, or ever,
It seemed so far, and little-like, and sad,
And I could sleep forever on Lilburn's shoulder,
Forever dark and quiet and day not come.

But close he leaned, and then his eyes were shining
Their deepest shine so dark, and he said: "Angel."

Said, "Angel, now you've told me all, now tell me,
Now didn't you like it some, and even to tell me?"
My cheeks got hot, like hot for shame, and suddenly
My breath was gone like I was dead, but my voice,
So strange, said: "Yes." And, oh, I wanted to sleep.

"But, Angel," Lilburn said, "just yesterday,
You were an angel and your hair was gold,
And golden stars in it, I put them there.
But now—"

               And sudden rose up from my side,
And stood up tall like he would fill the room,
And fill the house maybe, and split the walls,
And nighttime would come pouring in like flood,
And he was big all sudden, and no man
Was ever big like that, and way up there
His face was terrible and in its dark,
Like 'twas the darkness of an awful sky,
His eyes were shining, but they shone so dark.
And I was little—little then, and dry.

Listen—you know how when the locust goes
And his skin is left, a little shell of him,
All thin and dry and like a little ghost,
And light moves through it and the hollowness
So hollow it is nothing. That was me.

And way above swung Lilburn's face so dark,
And his voice said: "—but now I see when angels
Come down to earth, they step in dung, like us.
And like it."

And then he laughed right loud and long,
Then he was gone. And me there all alone,
While the fire died down and night came in, and me
All thin and dry, and through my hollowness
The dark and air might move and nothing be
But nothing to me in my hollowness.

BROTHER: God-a-Mighty, and you just never told me nothing.
He 'bused you wrong, and you laid up there a year
Before you broke and left him. And then, God-durn,
You moaned and jabbered, and never talked no sense.
You never told me how he done you wrong,
And how he 'bused you in the bed, and all.
If you told me, I'd stopped his clock long back.
Lewises, hell! Ain't nothing to a Lewis
Airy man ain't got, and him a man, and me—
And me, by God, I guess I'm much a man
As airy Lewis ever skinned a pecker,
Me—Billy Rutter—and by God, no man
Will do my sister dirty—

LAETITIA: Oh, your sister!
It's not your sister—me—you care about!

It's not for me, it's just yourself you care for,
To strut and brag, and maybe cut or kill.
Oh, you'd have killed my Lilburn if you knew,
Just to feel big because he was a Lewis,
And tell them in the tavern how it came,
And how no man would do your sister dirty.
Your sister!—Oh, it's not for love of me
You'd hurt my darling Lil—

And he, oh, God!
He's just like you, he took the golden stars
And put them in my hair and called me angel
And said he loved me, then did the thing he did.
Nobody loves nobody, they say, "Love,"
And love is the way lips move and a terrible sound,
And folks do what they do, and call it love.

But, oh, dear God, I swear I love him still.
I've got to try to love him, just to be.
But Lilburn rose up high, his face swung dark,
I thought the house would split and night flood in.
Said what he said, how angels step in dung,
And like it, too. Then gone, and me alone.
And gone three days, drunk in the settlement,
And beat the boy that Mother Lewis sent
To fetch him home—the nigger boy named George.

Poor George got back and stood inside the door.
He hugged the jamb to stand, so hurt and weak now,
Blood on his head, and down his poor face the blood,
And when a nigger bleeds, the blood is bright,
Brighter than white folks' blood. So he hung there,
And Mother Lewis looked, and cried, "Oh, George!"
He just hung there and wouldn't say a word.
And she, she stared, and ne'er a word, just staring
At George's face. Then reached out one finger, slow,
To touch the blood, like to believe it there.
And touched it.

LUCY: Yes, I touched it, and that instant
Of contact had all the terribleness of knowledge.
My mind was saying the pure and simple thing,
The sort of thing to live by and make the day good.
It was saying, simply: *This poor boy is hurt,*
Get water, bathe his blood, bind up the wound.
But I could not move to execute the good thing.
And that is strange—isn't it?—when the good thing
Lies clear and simple, but faculty is frozen.
Ah, had I got the water, bathed the wound,
Then everything might have been different, and the small
Obligation fulfilled had swayed the weight of the world.
But, no—and to this day I know no reason
Why then I could not act for the recognized good.

I stood and saw the black face blown with pain.
I saw the irrevocableness of the gaze fixed on me.
I saw my hand move out, weightless and witless and slow,
To glimmer white through the dark and thickening air.
And there was nothing else in the world left,
Like a wet sponge passed over a child's slate.

JEFFERSON: Yes, dear Sister, your hand reached out to touch
The brightness of violent blood, and in that moment
All values are abrogated in blankness, like the child's slate
                                        swabbed.
True. But no loss. For that's the slate
Where crooked figures crawl to compound error,
And the fond arithmetic of our sweetest human delusion
Flatter ferocity with virtue's sum.

That instant, then, dear Sister, you found yourself
At the moveless center of the cyclic storm,
And all life, all the cackle of voices, spun
Like wind around you in that idiot vortex.
But you were still, still and alone in that center
Where Nothing screams nothing.

                        Well, if you'd known
                                to define
The final reality, then you'd have struck,

Struck hard, and struck that black face whose pain
Was sweetness and reproach, and the blood-bright invitation.
Why not? What could the nigger brat have done?
Weak, sick, and hurt, afraid, a slave—
He'd see the blow, and wait, not even dodge,
For he, too, in that delicious and cataleptic focus, stands.
He stands, waits; and struck, will sink without a whimper.
And you, as your fist finds flesh, know a gush of wild joy,
And laugh ecstatically for the unimaginable relief, and—

LUCY: Hush, hush!

JEFFERSON: And laugh, and toss your head
                                        like a girl—

LUCY: Hush, brother, hush, there could have been nothing
                                        like that.
How could I strike poor George, him hurt already?
It was simply that I could not do the good thing
That was to be done, and had to stand and see
My hand move slow and glimmer in the dark air.

LAETITIA: It moved so slow, I just thought it would never—

LUCY: It was moving toward the instant of verification.
I knew that the blood there was but my evilest dream
And the bloody head before me but a dream,

And knew that if I reached and found but air
All sweet and empty like the breath of God,
I should wake up, and morning, morning and birdsong.
And so reached out—

JEFFERSON: And then, my Sister, touched—

LUCY: Yes, touched, and in that instant of contact, knew.
And cried out, "God!" And sudden, Time flowed back.
Flowed back and over. It whirled me like a flood.

LAETITIA: So she just fell down flat there on the floor.
We put her in the bed, and now sent Isham
Down to the settlement to fetch Lil home.
He came and stood all quiet at the bed-foot now,
Not drunk now, weak and pale, and her eyes came open,
But she could not speak—

LUCY: I knew my voice could not carry
Across that wide valley where the rain was falling.
It could not carry to his poor face that yearned.
And so I said nothing, knowing I had betrayed
My son and all the world's sweet need. And I died.

LAETITIA: Her breath just stopped, and she was dead,

                                        and we—
We didn't know. But Lilburn knew. His breath

Came sudden like a gasp, like in that second
What last breath she breathed out he'd sucked in him,
And had for his, to be in him, forever.

I turned and saw him—something on his face
Grew like a stain in water, and it spread,
And grew like darkness when the moon sinks down
And creeks and valleys dark, and the trees get black,
And grew like recollecting in the night
When you wake up cold and all you did seems awful,
Whatever it was, and shame to make you shake.
And so I saw it growing on his face,
And knew a-sudden what it was, and thought
All quiet inside me: *Look, he knows she's dead*
And we don't know—he knows because her dying
Is like his dying, too. And look, he's dead!
It was his own face dying that I saw,
And wanted to yell out and call his name,
Call, *Lilburn, please don't die, oh, Lilburn, Honey!*
For I forgot the thing he did to me,
That minute anyway, and loved him so.
But couldn't say a word, and my tears all frozen.

Then Doctor Charles, he leaned across the bed
And with his thumb and finger, sly and sleight,
Like you'd pick up a pin, he picked up slow
Her eyelid edge, and leaned the candle nigh.

And the eyeball just showed white in the candle flame.
He leaned and looked, like she was just anybody
Sore sick abed and him the doctor there,
And her not special, not his lawful wife
What always lay beside him all night long.
Then dropped the eyelid, and that little motion
Seemed awful to me, awful, like I'd scream,
Like with that little motion of his finger
He'd let her go, had let her fall, and she
Would fall forever in an awful dark
Where the stars don't come and even God's afraid.

He dropped the eyelid like you close a book,
But not a sound and all the reading done,
And stood up slow and set the candle by.
But then I saw his mouth was quivering,
Set in that face so sunken stone and still.
And no sound came. But then it came: "She's dead."

And Lilburn's breath came sharp, just like before.
Then Lil: "You're right, she's dead, and it was you—"
And stopped, and stared his Pappy in the face
With eyes all shining with a terrible shine.
"And it was you that killed her." He said that.

You've heard the stillness when the wind stops sudden.
You've heard the gunshot, then how sudden still

And a little wist of smoke all blue at the muzzle
And no wind stirs it, it so blue and pretty.
All frazzle-blue, and it never stirs at all.
The room was still. I saw his Pappy's face.
And the mouth did aim to move, but couldn't yet,
Nor soon, but I knew that when it did make words,
They'd be dead words, and so I thought: *Oh, God,
We're all dead here, and ain't no use to live.*

But the old man lifted up his hand. It shook.
He held it out like he would beg. He said:
"My boy, my boy." And that was all he said.
But Lilburn: "Oh, you killed her, you did that.
Brought her from Albemarle out here to die.
Oh, she loved Albemarle. You brought her here,
And woods are dark and the river stinks all summer,
And the world's a sty, and the world all stinks and stews,
Oh, she loved Albemarle—she was my mother—"
And Lil was crying then. The tears ran down.

I saw him cry, but couldn't stir nor budge.
He looked so little, who had been so big.
He looked so pale, whose face so dark and still.
He looked so weak, and him so strong and stout.
And made no sound, no sound. I saw the tears.
But I couldn't budge, nor lift a hand, nor move.

If I had budged, and him so wan and weak.
If just I touched him, just a finger-weight.

Or named his name, named, "Lil," so sweet and low.
Then all might different be, be nice, and all
Night long he'd lie and sleep inside my arm,
And dark 'twould be, and he would breathe so sweet,
And nothing happened ever, nor never dawn,
Nor rooster crow for meanness nor for spite
To end the dark where he will breathe so sweet,
Lying so sweet beside, and me smell his hair.
But I couldn't budge—

R. P. W.:   In other words, you couldn't,
To put the matter succinctly, forgive Lilburn.

LAETITIA: Forgive? Forgive? It wasn't not forgiving.
It wasn't anything—oh, what was it?
It was just I couldn't budge, and the world was ice.
It was Aunt Cat who—

R. P. W.:   It was Aunt Cat who what?

LAETITIA: When Lilburn cried, and all the tears ran down,
It was Aunt Cat—she stood and saw them run.
Then sudden was by him, quiet and quick like a breath,
And took his hand, and said: "Oh, Lil, my Honey—"
Like he was little, like the times gone by
When he was little and she nursed her Chile.

AUNT CAT: I nursed him good, and him my Chile and Honey.
Tiddy I give him, tiddy, and loved him good.

I rocked him soft, him stout and bouncin-glad,
And when his belly tight, I pat hit good,
So round and leetle, and I kiss him thar,
Sang, "Lil, my Lilly, Mammy's Baby-Bear."
And he done laugh to git me kiss and sing,
Sing fer the wind to blow and rock him soft,
Sing fer the moon to skeer the Bugaboo,
Sing fer the Cheer-kee never come not nigh
To skeer my punkin Little Baby-Bear,
And no Raw-Head-and-Bloody-Bones to come—
"Raw-Head, Raw-Head, doan come my Honey nigh."
Him sleep by then, and knowed I loved him good,
Fer in Virginny fer, him sleepin sound.

LAETITIA: The tears ran down, then Cat, she took his hand.
Said: "Lil, my Honey, come on, git to bed."
Said: "Chile." Said: "Chile." And him so drooped and slow.
Till nigh the door. Said: "Chile, yore Mammy's dead.
Miss Lucy gone and left her Chile to mourn,
But I'm yore Mammy, too. I give you tiddy."

He stopped then sudden-like, and swung round wild,
And stood. Then leaned and said, right in Cat's face:
"My mother's dead. I sucked your milk, but now—"

And stopped.

And Cat said: "Chile."

And then he said,

"But now I'd puke it out, the last black drop,
I'd puke it out—oh, God! my mother's dead."

Then she put hands on him, and said: "Oh, Chile!"
But he jerked back, said: "Take your black hand off!"
And said: "What's yours in me, I'll spit it out!"
And then he spat. He spat there on the floor.
And the room all still, and the dead one on the bed.
And Cat, she cried. She cried, it hurt her so.

R. P. W.: Yes, it was monstrous, what he did, all right.
But in a strange way somewhat justified.
Oh, no—not justified. I don't mean that.
Nothing can justify the essential cruelty
Of what he said. But Aunt Cat asked for it.

LAETITIA: She loved him, that was all.

R. P. W.: She loved him, sure.
But that's not all, for even love's a weapon,
Or can be a weapon. Let's take the situation.
Now anybody raised down home—down South—
Will know in his bones what the situation was.
For all those years Aunt Cat had fought in silence
For Lilburn's love, for possession of her Chile,
With the enemy, the rival, Lucy Lewis.

The rival had the armament and power:
The natural mother, warm and kind—and white.
The rival whose most effective armament
Is the bland assumption that there is no struggle—
Nor can be—between the white love and the black.
It is a struggle, dark, ferocious, in the dark,
For power—for power empty and abstract,
But still, in the last analysis, the only
Thing worth the struggle.

                This much Aunt Cat knows,
And knows she has one weapon, only one,
And the weapon is love. So when the mother's dead,
Cat's sympathy and love is proclamation and triumph
Over the fallen adversary. Then no wonder
That Lilburn struck in rage, and outrage, back.
But still, Cat loved him, and that love is valid,
And to be prized. This isn't cynicism.
And Lilburn—

LAETITIA: Oh, Lilburn walked the woods, and it was dark.
We called and called, but his dog barked far away.
Then late, so late, I lay in my bed and waited,
And in the dark I knew how Time moved by
Nor never knows your name nor looks at you,
No matter who you be, nor your name, in the dark.

Then Lilburn came, came out the woods and darkness.
He came to my bed and laid his head dark down,

And on my shoulder lay so sweet, and said:
"Oh, Tishy, Tishy, oh, my mother's gone."
And tears came out, and wet me through my gown.
Then I wanted to feel something, but just couldn't,
Or felt too many things, all different,
And that was worse than not to feel a thing,
And my hand would pat his head there in the dark,
But every pat a lie. But my hand still patted.
Can you tell me why I never felt a thing?

R. P. W.: What could it have changed, a gush of feeling?
Both you and Lucy choose to torture that question,
To assume that some difference in tone or gesture
Would have changed—

LUCY: Oh, no, not tone, not gesture, but
The heart, a difference in the heart, and all
Might have been changed—

JEFFERSON: Nothing would change nothing!
For Lilburn is an absolute of our essential
Condition, and as such, would ingurgitate
All, and all you'd give, all hope, all heart,
Would only be disbursed down that rat hole of the ultimate
                                        horror.

Nothing would change.

R. P. W.: Well, nothing did change.

Lilburn was Lilburn, and the year drove on.

They buried Lucy Lewis in the yard,

And the year drove on. Winter. And from the Dakotas

The wind veers, gathers itself in ice-glitter

And star-gleam of dark, and finds the long sweep of the valley.

A thousand miles and the fabulous river is ice in the starlight.

The ice is a foot thick, and beneath, the water slides black

like a dream,

And in the interior of that unpulsing blackness and

thrilled zero

The big channel-cat sleeps with eye lidless, and the brute face

Is the face of the last torturer, and the white belly

Brushes the delicious and icy blackness of mud.

But there is no sensation. How can there be

Sensation when there is perfect adjustment? The blood

Of the creature is but the temperature of the sustaining flow:

The catfish is in the Mississippi and

The Mississippi is in the catfish and

Under the ice both are at one with God.

Would that we were!

But far north the geat conifers darkly bend and unburden

The cope and dignity of snow, and the stridor

Rises to anguish. What does the oak say?

The oak stands on a headland above an enormous curve of

the river.

It has stood there a hundred years. The trunk is iron.

The powerful boughs that crook and lift are iron, and lifeless.
The oak's comment is anguish, but the oak stands.
The oak is Jacob, and all night in anguish wrestles the

incessant

And pitiless angel of air. The stars are arctic and
Their gleam comes earthward down uncounted light-years

of disdain,

And on the exposed headland the oak heaves,
And in radius of more than a thousand miles the continent
Glitters whitely in starlight like a great dead eye of ice.
The wind is unceasing, and the stars likewise.

Why do we feel the necessity to linger on this scene?
The answer, I hazard, is paradoxical.
We feel that the force now driving Lilburn on
Is but part of the unleashed and unhouseled force of Nature,
Mindless, irreconcilable, absolute:
The swing of the year, the thrust of Time, the wind.
But we also feel a need to leave that house
On the dark headland, and lift up our eyes
To whatever liberating perspective,
Icy and pure, the wild heart may command,
To escape the house, escape the tightening coil
And mathematical constriction: and so the glimmering

night scene and storm under

The incalculable and distant disdain of starlight, serve,

therefore,

As an image of lethal purity, the incessant

And whirling dream of desperate innocence,
The infatuate glitter of the land of Platonic ice.
It is an image to free us from the human trauma,
And the wind drives unremitting, and the oak will bend.

Southward, the deep intimacy of thicket not yet shudders.
In the icy and abstract stillness, the last burr that clung
On the chestnut bough, surrenders, the last haw-fruit,
In the silence, falls, and what berry of dogwood the possum

spared

Falls now, in the hour, past pain, of the relaxed tendon.

The first tremor, no gust yet, is here.
By creeks, in the bottoms, dry cane, with ice-glaze, shakes.
It clashes thinly in the glittering infinitude of night.
There is no ear to hear. Now the wind, and the oak will bend.

After a thousand miles the wind shakes the walls of

the house.

The logs of the house are deep-notched, and the house is set
On stone, but the structure shudders in the big blast.
The candle-flame shudders on the wick. The wind
Has found the chimney now, sparks eddy the hearth.
"Isham," says Lilburn, "shove me that God-damned jug."

And Isham shoves the jug, and Lilburn drinks.
The candle-flame now steadies on the wick.
They are alone. Laetitia lies upstairs.

Lies in the big bed and rarely leaves it now.
The slaves are in their quarters, snug as varmints,
Save George, who drowses by the kitchen fire,
Waiting to help his master up to bed.
And, as for Dr. Lewis, he is gone.
Back to Virginia, back where—

CHARLES: Not that it mattered.
Can it matter where wanders the emptiness of air?
Wind, force without body, word without
Meaning, accident without essence.
Even in that time when still I paid my taxes,
Transacted business, gorged and voided bowels,
And was an identity defined in the temporal eye—
Even then, as I recollect, I was sometimes surprised
To see that my boot left print in dust or damp earth.
To Kentucky I had come to seek my reality.
But in Kentucky I had lost the one person
To whom I was real. But the loss, I must confess,
Was ambiguous. There was, of course, my sorrow.
Relief, also. Relief that I was no longer
In need to strive to be worthy of her love:
Ah, the terrible burden of love!

                         We buried her
Alone in the wild earth, and my heart said: "Oh, Lucy,
My Lucy, rot to nothingness, enter

The dark and depth of nothingness, rot,
And rot quickly, into the absolute oblivion,
That in nothingness we may at long last love
In the appropriate mutuality, nothing
To nothing."

And turned away and took the long
Road home, over the mountains, far away,
And in that action equivalently said:
And may my seed rot and the fruit of your womb.
I leave them unto darkness and the dark land.
I have looked in the eyes of my first-born son and have seen
The landscape of shadow and the shore of night.
Let him fulfill my destiny. Farewell.
And took my leave, and waited for the end.

R. P. W.: So Lilburn's now alone. They have left him now,
Mother and father, wife, and old Aunt Cat.
For if his wife and Cat are in the house,
Their faces turn, they drift like shadow past,
And Lilburn knows that he's repudiated.
There's Isham—he is there, I'd near forgot;
But can Isham mitigate such loneliness?
There's some excuse, therefore, for Lilburn's wild wail
Of loneliness, when he first appeared to us,
And his complaint of desertion in the dark.
But we may say, with logic, it was he
Who did the repudiating, who cast forth

Them all. That's true. But even as we say so,
We must remember that always the destroyer
It is who has most need of love: therefore destroys.
And in the unity of life remember
That destruction's but creation gone astray,
That life and death both enter by a wound,
And that in the eternal paradox of powers
The oldest ritual instructs us how
Pelasgian bull and Etruscan ram are felled
By fang of panther or the lion's paw;
And the sad god rises in season past the pathos.
And I once read in Bernard of Clairvaux
How the wicked man, even in wickedness, but seeks God,

after all.

JEFFERSON: But the fact is always the fact—

R. P. W.:   And the year

drove on.

It drives past the dire solstice, and death of the heart.
Drives past the weeping for innocence, and the childhood lost,
And the lost comfort of the nocturnal whisper.
Now is the hour of iron: accept the obligation,
And the sap of compassion withdraws uttermost inward
To sleep in the secret chamber of the deep root of being.
Where is that chamber? And the year drives on.

And now is a new year: 1811.
This is the *annus mirabilis*. Signs will be seen.

The gates of the earth shall shake, the locked gate
Of the heart be stricken in might by the spear-butt.
Men shall speak in sleep, and the darkling utterance
Shall wither the bride's love, and her passion become
But itch like a disease: scab of desire.
Hoarfrost shall lie thick in bright sun, past season, and
twitch like fur.

The call of the owl shall discover a new register.
When ice breaks, the rivers shall flood effortlessly,
And the dog-fox, stranded on the lost hillock,
Shall bark in hysteria among the hazel stems.
Then the bark shall assume a metronomic precision.
Toward the end, silence. The first water coldly fingers
The beast's belly. Then silence. He shudders, lets
The hind quarters droop beneath the icy encroachment.
But the head holds high. The creature shivers again,
And the rigid muzzle triangulates the imperial moon.
Until the spasm, the creature stares at the moon
With the aggrieved perplexity of a philosopher.

Sullen, the waters withdraw. Mud crusts the high
White boughs of the sycamore. Slime crusts the creek-flats.
It is green like velvet. Sickness begins in June.
Strong men die willingly. Only the old
Fight for life. Stertorous breath shakes the pole-shanty.
Dog-days, and stars fall, and prayers have ceased.
Men had come West in hope. This is the West.

Therefore what more is there for man to hope for?
The arrogant comet shoulders the old constellations.
It comes too late, men now past fear or wonder:
From clearing or keelboat only a dull eye observes.
Night after night and it sheds a twilight of shuddering **green**
Over the immensity of forest. The beasts
Of the forest participate in the peculiar dislocation.
Habit and courage of kind change, and lust
Out of season, and lust for strange foods, as when
Rome shook with civil discord, and therefore the **beasts,**
Augustine says, kept not their order, for the wild
Clang of that untunement echoed in all things.
Strange reports are in the valley of the Mississippi.
Squirrels flee South, but cannot cross the Ohio.
They drown there, by thousands. Their bodies **bloat on the**
sand bars.

The wild pigeon migrates early this year.
Their droppings have a strange odor, and men
With nausea reject this once-esteemed fowl.
Signs are diversely read. There is rumor of war.
The worst is to come yet, when the earth shall shake.

But not yet, and life proceeds at Rocky Hill.
All spring you can look from the bluff-head, and see **far,**
Far off, how the waters stand on the flat land.
The waters subside too late for corn. But grass,
Sparse and tentative, sprigs the raw earth

Of Lucy's grave, and Lilburn comes from the house
To stand and stare at the spot. He comes softly,
And though it is in the broad light of day,
Comes like a thief, or lecher, setting the foot down
With secrecy ominous on the unsounding earth.
He does not understand what is big in his heart,
Nor why something like guilt oppresses his breathing,
Nor why there should be a nagging pain in the left groin.
It has nagged him for days. He must have strained himself.
He has been with a slut at the settlement and wonders
If somehow he strained himself. He was drunk and cannot
Recall clearly. But as for the guilt he feels,
If it is guilt, it is not guilt for that.
Laetitia has refused him. Well, that's that.

Now he stands by the new grave, raw, and the pain nags.
April: the grave here six months now, and the grass
Now makes the first green gesture of reclamation.
On the mound, slightly eroded by winter and delicately
Veined by trickle of water in the months past,
Each blade of grass is isolated, and pale
With April's pale perfection, and each blade
Protruding, lost, from that earth's intolerable rawness,
Seems an independent project, with its own value,
And is intolerable. He stares at the grass,
And each single, identifiable blade is intolerable,
And is an agony. He cannot bear

The sight of the grass. He knows that when the grass
Comes back with sweetness and vernal mitigation,
Then he will be deprived of something, something
He cannot name, of some essential reality.
He craves the sight of the wounded earth. He craves
The pain, the sorrow, the oppression of breath, that wound
And exacerbation of earth. Ah, that's reality!
If the grass comes back, then what, what, will be left?
Nothing, oh, nothing: *emptiness*. His heart
Floods dear with desolation. His eyes brim.
Why does he suffer and understand nothing?
Were we in his place, we should surely understand.
For we are instructed in the mystery of the heart,
But he is not. His breath is difficult.

At this moment now, the favorite hound approaches.
The creature approaches silent on the sod,
Tail down, or wagging slightly, the pace slow.
The hound stands by the master, and the mournful
Head lifts to gaze with uncritical sympathy
Upon the unformulable distress of the master.
The hound licks the down-hung hand of the master.
The master looks down and for an instant graciously
Accepts the fact. But the tongue's sweetness on flesh
And the gaze of brute affection touch some trigger
Deep in his being, some reflex of desperation.
Lilburn kicks the hound savagely in the side.

He cannot help it; the act surprises himself.
But the next act does not surprise. The hound
Has been bowled over, yelps, but does not flee.
It crawls, drag-belly on the grass, to Lilburn.
It knows there has been some terrible mistake
And would rectify all, by love. There has been no mistake.
This time Lilburn kicks with the greatest deliberation.
The hound shuts eyes, and shivers; takes the blow;
Then flees. Flees now, and Lilburn stands enrapt,
While joy and sorrow deep contend and gleam
Down what new arch and arch and vista inward ever.
He stands, dazed, in the April sunlight of the Year of Wonder.

Later, in shame, he seeks the hound. The hound
Forgives him, licks his hand, but Lilburn worries
Why he can feel no joy. He would like to feel
The ineffable joy of the soul's restoration.
That night he strikes a slave. The slave's transgression
Had not been great. The slave had broken a cup
That Lucy Lewis habitually had used
For morning tea. The thing spoke no great value,
And the breaking, too, was clearly accidental.
The slave protests, for in the Lewis house
All discipline has been by kindness and in
Each day's easy justice. Protests: that's his mistake.
Next morning whipped, and that with Lilburn by

To count the strokes, assess the proper force.
It's George again, a boy just turned sixteen.
Then Lilburn rides down to the settlement
To take his joram; and scarcely round the bend
When George lights out. His world's all upside down.
Can't stand it. Cuts for the woods. The second mistake:
For where, in those days, could a nigger run?
Starvation or the scalping knife, that's all.
So belly-growl or reflection on the transience
Of the human topknot might send the fellow home.
That is, if still he had topknot to noggin.
This one came home, hungry, to take his stripes.

And so things start: Violence breeds cunning, and cunning
Violence, and the first cup in innocence broken
Is succeeded by a dozen broken by design.
But who has broken them? Nobody knows.
They just aren't there any more, on hook or shelf.
Spoons disappear. Where do they go? Who knows?
It doesn't matter to the Negroes now
It's Ole Miss's cup—Miss Lucy's cup or spoon.
They'd loved Miss Lucy—or if the word *love*
Sounds too much like old Thomas Nelson Page
To sit easy on our stomachs salivated with modernity,
Then we can say that in the scale of subordination,
The black, that victim of an obsolescent

Labor system (we can't, you see, just say
"Immoral labor system," as I'd near done,
For that wouldn't be modern, except for people
Who want things both ways)—well, to start again:
The victims of the obsolescent labor system
Had been conditioned, by appeals to the ego,
To identify themselves with the representative
Of the superordinate group, i.e., the mistress—
In other words, they liked her "tol-bul well."
Might say: "Miss Lucy, she ain't done so bad."
Might say: "Ole Miss, she know a nigger feel."
In other words, the humanity of the poor slave
Could rise above the system's corrupting arrangement,
Ignorance, resentment, slyness, sloth, despair,
The limen of anguish and the bar of rage,
To recognize the human hope of another person;
And if that is not love, then it's something better.

Well, they had loved Miss Lucy, and no doubt
Would have defended all her spoons against
The Powers of Darkness and Old Scratch Himself
With reasonable loyalty, if it came to a tight,
But now—now things are different—she is dead.
And do they come to hate her, too, that instant
The cup splits on the stone, or the spoon whitely
Wavers and glimmers to die in the dark deep of water?
They'd have to hate her, too, to justify.

Yes, all is different now. Things disappear,
And Lilburn feels a constriction at his temples.
Spoons, cups. Where do they go? Who knows?
A man just can't keep track of things like that.
A woman might. Laetitia, for example,
If she weren't sick and lying off upstairs,
Eyes on the ceiling, in her sad dream.
Yes, any woman might. She might surprise
Dish-washing or table-setting, and make her audits,
And still not be regarded as a monster in the kitchen.
They'd say: "Ole Miss—you know, she jes lak dat."
The Negroes could say that about her and accept
Her cantankerousness as part of the uncomfortable furniture
Of the world, and nothing more.

                              But in a man
It's monstrous, out of nature, for a man
Just doesn't know the rules of such a game.
If in the middle of the afternoon,
Lilburn, just day-drunk and not night-drunk yet
(Day-drunk—a stage known only by a slight
Up-twitching of the left corner of the mouth,
Not quite enough to show the jaw's canine)—
Well, if Lilburn comes to the kitchen now, and with enormous
Deliberation surveys that obscure cave
Where, in the shadow, eye-whites roll and gleam,
And says: "I want to see my mother's spoons!"

If he does that, it disturbs the kitchen's dignified
And submarine peace, and the white eyeballs gleam in

shadow.

"God damn it, fetch 'em now!" he says. They fetch 'em.
Always one less. Always somebody gets hurt.

But Lilburn most. He feels that something, something
Just terrible, is happening to his mother.
He feels that they are making the grass come back
On that raw earth of her grave. He feels that they
Are making the flesh fall off her bones, and changing
The expression of her face. He tries to stop it.
He tries, but it seems that nothing he can do
Can impede that perfidy of the secret hand,
Black thumb on china white, on silver, the black
Finger fastidiously plucking flesh from bone.
He does not see these images, he only
Feels them, and feels always the eyes that spy—

JEFFERSON: Spy—yes, they spy—they spy from the shadow.
They spy from the darkest corner of the hall,
They serve you the dish and stand with face blandly
Averted, but sidewise that picklock gaze has triggered
The tender mechanism of your destructive secret.
Oh, they've surprised you
At meat, at stool, at concupiscence; and with sardonic

detachment

Have even inspected your face while you turned inward
To the most soul-searching meditation. And when
You turn inward, at the heart's darkest angle you meet
The sly accusation and the shuttered gleam
Of that sidelong eye.

R. P. W.:   I begin to think
You're finding some sort of justification for Lilburn.

JEFFERSON: But listen and you can hear nothing, their feet

come

Softly, and their feet come softlier than silence,
And innocence will avail nothing—I tried
To be innocent, but the eyes—

R. P. W.:   Were there. And you lived
In the lean, late years by the skill of some colored mechanics,
Nailmakers I think, that luckily you'd trained up.
Well, this is impertinent, but to build Monticello,
That domed dream of our liberties floating
High on its mountain, like a cloud, demanded
A certain amount of black sweat.

JEFFERSON: I lived in the world.
Say that. But say, too, that I tried to envisage
The human possibility.

R. P. W.:   Oh, I grant that.
And I wasn't trying just now to jockey you
Into the position of justifying your kinsman.
Sure, I know well—who doesn't know down home?—
The intolerable eye of the sly one, and the foot
Soundless, and the sibilant confabulation below
The threshold of comprehension.

> What the hell did you say?
> Me, Boss? You mean me?
> Who the hell you think I mean, you black bastard?
> Me, Boss?
> Yes, you—what the hell was that you said?
> Boss, I did'n say nothin.

It is always nothing, but always there around you:
And in the deep vessel of self now the dark
Lees and dregs are disturbed, uncoil now, and rise
To murk the clear, rational ichor of innocence.
No use to say now you've dealt justly with individuals
Or held the most advanced views on the race question.
Do you think the Dark Inquisitor can be deflected
By trivialities like that?

JEFFERSON: Do you—
Do you think now to instruct me on that point?
I'd said there's no defense of the human definition.
And as for Lilburn, it's you who would defend him.

R. P. W.: I'd not defend him but I'd like to know
Exactly how it was he came to the hour
That is indefensible—for somehow we know
That that last hour indefensible,
When the stars sweat and the dear toad weeps in the hole,
Is but the sum of all the defensible hours
We have lived through.

JEFFERSON: No, Lilburn is Lilburn, as you said—

R. P. W.: But I'm not sure I meant it just that way,
Not in your tone of voice, at least. For if the thing
Accomplished would seem to accomplish only its own
Inevitability, and the thing that exists
Would seem to fulfill only its own being,
And to be but the Q.E.D. of a fatal sorites,
Yet the accomplished was once the unaccomplished
And the existing was once the non-existing,
And that transition was the agony of will
And anguish of option—or such it seems
To any man who has striven in the hot day and glare of
                                        contingency
Or who has heard the breath of darkness stop
At the moment of revelation. And such it seems
To all who would lay a strong hand strongly on life,
And as for the others, let us wish them well
In the ineluctable sterility of their various sanatoria

Where all the light is like a light from snow,
And hope that there's always somebody to change the

bedpans.

No, that is wicked. We know we all need grace,
And pity too, and charity is the index
Of strength, and the worship of strength is but the index
Of weakness, but, by God, that's still no reason
To regard all history as a private alibi-factory
And all God's gleaming world as a ward for occupational

therapy.

For if responsibility is not
The thing given but the thing to be achieved,
There is still no way out of the responsibility
Of trying to achieve responsibility.
So, like it or lump it, you are stuck.

No, I'd not defend Lilburn, no, not that,
But once we have him there's no use to condemn,
And I've got enough of morbid curiosity
To want to know how Lilburn came to the last.
Know's not the word. *Guess* will do better here.
For even Lilburn couldn't know—knew only
The tightening concatenation of need and terror
And the incredibleness of each deed done
In the aghast logic of compulsion,
And unreality grows round him like a fog
And he must strike through the fog, strike hard to find

Contact with something real, something solid,
Something that will, perhaps, scream out its reality
And in that scream affirm, at last, poor Lilburn's own.
For all we all ask in the end is that:
Reality.

But back to Lilburn. And there's Isham, too.
Young Isham who just loved Big Bubber so.
That's what Laetitia said. And we could make a guess
That Lilburn knew it, and could not bear to be loved.
And strange: For love was all he asked, yet love
Is the intolerable accusation of guilt
To all the yearning Lilburns who cannot love,
So must destroy who loves, and achieve at last
The desiderated and ice-locked anguish of isolation.

Well, he's near done that now, Lilburn I mean:
Mother and Father gone, Laetitia sick
And still and white-lipped when he comes to her,
Aunt Cat with sulks and sulls and her deep grief.
The slaves all slow with hate like a disease,
And even the hound in the sweet midst of fawning
With a wary eye on Lilburn's right boot.
At least, so Lilburn thinks, and feels the twitch
Of nerve and muscle in the right leg.
He shoves the beast away. He doesn't want,
He honestly doesn't want, to kick the hound,

But the agonizing sweetness of possibility
Grows, now grows like love, so he yells out:
"Fetch me the bottle, George, and damn it, fast!"
Maybe the bottle will help whatever's wrong.
George comes, eyeballs set sidewise, hand unsure.
And Lilburn stares at him like something new,
Stares till the sweat runs down from out the kinks,
And in a whisper, vibrant as joy, says:
"You're sure one slow, ass-dragging, blue-gum bastard."
And then: "Get out!" George gets. And Lilburn turns
To Isham and—

ISHAM: Yeah, yeah, he turned to me!
Me sitting there, and said: "I don't know why,
I just can't stand that slinking nigger bastard.
Looks like he just does something to me now,
Something I just can't stand." So takes a drink.
And me, I don't say nothing.

R. P. W.:   What's there to say?

ISHAM: And Lil, he looks at me like it's not me,
And says: "You just sit there, and nothing said."
And me: "Just nothing sort of came to say."
And him: "Whose side you on now, his or mine?"
And me: "Now, Bubber, listen—look here now—"
Then Lilburn: "Damn you, so you take his side,

You love that slinking nigger better'n me,
And me your brother, and I was good to you,
But you—you love a blue-ass nigger better'n me."
And jumped up straight, and hit the table hard.
"Bubber!" I said. And sudden, he was gone.

R. P. W.: Up to his old tricks still. But tricks, no doubt,
He didn't invent. We've met those tricks before:
"Whose side you on?" Or: "You're against me, too."
There's nothing to wait for then. Then all is over.

ISHAM: Yeah, he was mean sometimes, but that was Lil.
He'd hurt your feelings, but you had to reckon
It was his blues that made him, not he meant to.
That's what our mother said: "That's only Lil,
It's just the way he is, and not he means to.
He means no harm, not with you his Little Brother."
But when—

R. P. W.:   When what?

ISHAM: Oh, when it happened, then—

R. P. W.: You mean the meat-house?

ISHAM: No, I mean the last,
And how it wasn't me, it wasn't me,
That did the last thing.

R. P. W.:   That did the last what?

ISHAM: Hell, it's no use to name the last thing now.
You got to tell it how it came on slow,
Then of a sudden there, like a gunshot—
Yeah, like a gunshot—yeah, and Lilburn's face
There of a sudden staring at me strong,
And keeps on staring, and my lips won't move
To say, "Oh, Bubber!" and just to tell him, tell him,
But now I just can't say it, and I can't tell him
I never meant to do it, and he stands and stares,
But it's already happened—

                              Already, while far off,
Far off in the woods some son-of-a-bitch of a bird
Keeps singing his crazy son-of-a-bitch of a head off,
Like I didn't have a thing not better to do
Than listen to that son-of-a-bitch sing his head off.
But there's no noise, not one, and in the woods
Every leaf hangs still now, and just that bird sings,
And so I stand and Lilburn stares at me
All strange and strong, and maybe if I listen
To that son-of-a-bitch of a bird for just a second,
Can listen hard enough and just forget,
Then maybe nothing has happened—but Lil—then Lilburn—
And then he falls.

R. P. W.:   It was your own suggestion.
To be more systematic, first things first,
And let whatever the deuce this last thing is
Go till the last. Suppose I summarize.
Correct me when you wish. Well, to begin:
When Lucy's dead, things go from bad to worse.
Defending spoons then, Lilburn beats the people.
George gets the roughest, Lilburn can't stand George.
That's what he says. Yet George is his body-servant.
George tries the woods, comes back, gets beat again.
The drink gets worse—there's always been enough.
The isolation Lilburn wants draws on.
You're left—alone with that brother whom you love so well.

ISHAM: But Lil—if you could know him, how he was—
He was a man and God-a-Mighty strong,
And laughed and rollicked when he wasn't blue,
And slapped me on the back and named me "Ishey"—
"Old Ishey-Boy," he'd say, "Old Ishey-Boy"—
And the time he wrestled in the settlement—
Yeah, let me tell you, I'll tell you how it was.
You've seen a bear, how stout, well, that was Lil.
You've seen a bobcat, sly, well, that was Lil.
And a painter fast, to jump and come again,
And come again, and still his face was smiling,
And teeth a-shine, and laughed out loud and long

To grab that man and heave him up sky-high.
Then sudden-quick he cracked him on the ground.
You heard the crack. And all the folks all yelled.
They yelled Lil's name, and I said marvel-slow—
So young I was—"Why, that's my Bubber there!"
'Twas like I prayed, me just a little bastard—
You know how 'tis when you're still just a sprig—
And asked the Lord to make me big like my brother,
And make him love me, like I loved him then.

R. P. W.: Well, that was perfect preparation, sure,
For the dolorous sequel when the years drew on,
And you were there, bound hand and foot, for Lilburn
To quarrel with, abuse, humiliate,
But never too much, always the right degree,
So you could be restored to your brother,
And always all, each act, in the name of love.
He would not alienate you, not completely.
It's cat-and-mouse. He saves you for some inescapable
Truth-dazzled hour when the heart shall burst
In gouts of glory—hallelujah!—like a flower.
He awaits the hour of the Pentecostal intuition.

He does not know what hour, but he knows it will come.
He does not know what Truth,
Nor knows its name,
But knows it will come,

And so abides that beauty,
And therefore would merely reserve you
And plays with alienation,
After each act of alienation, plucks
You back,
Restores you,
Draws you on
Deeper and deeper in that darkling thicket
Of his dark dream,
And fades before you ever,
With sad face smiling and the beckoning hand,
With pity in the smile, and the lips soundlessly
Will part to say,
"Oh, Ishey, Little Ishey!"
And fades before you. Goes. Now comes again,
And all the forest darker swells beyond,
And thorns, like guilt, will tear you as you plunge,
And cobwebs fetter you and fold your face
In terror of their weak tenacity.

Ah, deeper, deeper, has the dark no center?
Ah, deeper! has the night no moment poised
Before the stroke, systole and diastole,
Where hope is happy and the dark hangs down
Like benediction and you smell the grass—
Remember how, in the dark, dew smells on the grass?—
Or was it like that?

ISHAM: There's just no way to reckon
How a thing happens to you. It just happens.

R. P. W.: And summer passed, and sickness walked the land.
Crops failed, and Nature creaked on its hinges
Like an old shed door at night when the wind shifts.
And the Terrible Year bloomed its malignancy,
And you and Lilburn sat all night by the jug,
Night after night, and what one time had been
Intolerable became bread of the heart.
The comet has come, and gone, dispensing its splendor.
And now December 15, 1811.
Do you recall exactly what happened that day?

ISHAM: Why, nothing—nothing happened—just a day.
But three days sooner, something happened then.
'Twas George came back again from running off.

R. P. W.: I'd near forgot—yes, Lil had beat

George again.

ISHAM: Just a fool nigger. Looks like he'd a-learned.
Learned something anyway. If you're scared of the woods,
Don't run to the woods, get scared, and then come back
To take a worse hiding. That fool, all sick and hungry,
Came back for his hiding. That's three days before.
But the day came now.

But it was just a day,
Another day and dark a-settling down,
And nothing happened, nothing, like the world was tired,
So many years, and time, all passed away,
And fire on the hearth now low. You chunk it up.
And there's not much to say, just sitting there,
Lil yelled for his jug. George came, and brought the jug.
It's night by now.

R. P. W.:   Let now the night descend
With all its graduated terrors,
And in its yearning toward absoluteness now amend
The impudent daylight's velleities, and errors,
And let the dark's most absolute shame
Amend the day's finicking shamelessnesses,
And in that dark let the absoluteness of hate's dark flame
Consume, like pitch-pine, the heart that had longed for
                    love's timid and tentative caresses.

For all life lifts and longs towards its own name,
And toward fulfillment in the singleness of definition,
So in the dark now let
The dark flame lift, unfolding like a flower,
And let the darkest flower bloom like flame
Whose beauty hangs unmoving in our eye,
For all achieved perfection can only proclaim
The thrust toward timelessness, in Time.

So let the dark stalk stand
To unfold foliage convolute like flame.
And slowly now it swells
From the blind nutriment of Lilburn's heart—
That rich detritus of all History,
Muck, murk, and humus, and the human anguish,
And human hope,
And let lianas writhe,
And the valved calyx of the parasite
Inhale, with soundless pulse and precision,
The exciting foetor
Of darkness,
And from the fronded boles of Time
A night depends that knows no dawn, nor hour
Dappled by daylight, and sun never comes.

Well, in this period of the final tumescence
From what fat oubliettes of inwardness
Let Lilburn speak.
What did he say, Isham?

ISHAM: He asked me did I really love our mother.

R. P. W.: And you, what did you say?

ISHAM: I said I loved her,
And once at night dreamt how she sang to me.
And he said, "Stop!" And jumped up from his chair.

Then looked at me just like he hated me,
And said: "Now what the hell made you tell me that?"

And me: "It's true—I dreamt she sang to me,
Like I was little and she came and leaned."

And him: "It's just a lie—you never dreamed it.
It's me, I dream that dream, I guess I know—
She comes and leans and smiles like years long back,
And I can hear already, sweet and low,
But not a sound. And then her face, it's dead—
Oh, it's a lie she came and sang to you!"

And me: "But, Lil, it's just a dream I had."
And him: "It's just a lie—why sing to you?"
And then so pitiful it hurt my heart:
"Oh, Ishey—Ishey—she never sings to me."
And me: "But look, it's nothing but a dream!"
And him: "She's dead, and black dirt chokes her singing,
But if you loved her—oh, if you did—you'd stop 'em."
And me: "Stop who?"

　　　　　　And him: "You God-damn fool,
And blind to boot, to watch 'em every day,
And like they killed her over every day.
I'll tell you how, if you're a blind damn fool.
Listen—" And leans: "And all the things she loved,

The things she brought from Albemarle out here,
From Albemarle, where she was happy once—
Listen, they steal her spoons!
The cup she drank from, say who broke that now?
They tear the sheets where she lay down to die—
But you don't care—oh, you, you never loved her!"
And he leans at me—

R. P. W.:   And leans, and his heart knows
That the night grows big with possibility,
And Lilburn knows that now is the time to know,
If ever, if you, his Little Brother Isham,
Do truly love him and will take his hand.
And now leans slow at you—

ISHAM: Yeah, leans at me,
And stares at me, and points up to the shelf,
And says: "You see our mother's pitcher there—
All gold and flowers, the one she loved so much
From Albemarle, and set up high to see?"
I see the pitcher, and I see his face.
"Listen," he says, "they're waiting now, they're waiting.
They bide a time to break it when they can."
There's nothing now to say. I see his eyes.

He stepped back quick and took the pitcher down:
"That's what they'll do—and you, oh, if you loved her—"

He stands and holds the pitcher in his hands,
And stares like he would eat it with his eyes.
Then jerks his head up quick. And yells: "You, George!"
And George comes from the kitchen where he's squatting
Afore the fire, and snoozing like a nigger.
Comes footing slow. And stands. His eyes roll.

Now things get queer. I never hated George.
Before, I mean. Him just another nigger.
But now to see him standing there so weak,
And frail to fall, and how his eyes were rolling
Like one more nigger sick and nigh to gone,
It looked to me there wasn't a thing but hate
Inside me, and to hate that nigger George
For being so God-damn mean-weak was nothing
But sweet joy.

        And Lilburn's voice way off
Was saying how he needed some fresh water
To mix his whisky, and for George to go
Down to the spring and fetch it. Then I knew.
Then Lilburn shoved the pitcher there to George.
I knew he would. George took it, and my breath
Came short. I just can't say: "Look, George, don't take it!"
I can't say that. You see, I want him to.
And Lilburn's voice, far off, is saying still:
"That is my mother's pitcher, and she loved it.

If anybody breaks my mother's pitcher,
I just can't say what'll happen to that nigger.
Now, git!"

       And George gets nigh the door, but Lilburn,
He says: "Wait now!" And turns to me: "Now, Ishey,
Why don't you wake our people up and bring 'em
Up to the meat-house, make 'em make a fire.
We don't want folks a-catching cold round here.
And let 'em sing, maybe, and pat some juba,
To pass the time till me and George get back."

Then turns. Then stops. Says, "Ah." Then from the shelf
He reaches up and hands the pistols down.
He gives them to me. He laughs and says: "These niggers—
You know how niggers are, they get excited.
Just take these tricks, in case they get excited.
And me—I'll get myself some evening air.
I'll go with George. He's scared of the dark, sometimes.
But George, you're safe tonight. I'm right behind you.
I won't let Raw-Head scare pore little George."
Then they are gone, Lil walking soft behind,
And saying soft: "That pitcher—if you break it—"

R. P. W.: And so you went down to the meat-house?

ISHAM: I roused our people out, all but Aunt Cat.
I roused 'em out and made 'em come with me

And build the fire and get the meat-house **ready**.

R. P. W.: Ready for what?

ISHAM: For what? I didn't **know**.
If I had known, maybe I couldn't done it.
And yet I knew, and that's so God-durn **queer**,
How knowing and not knowing are one **thing**,
And that one thing is just what's going to **happen**
Anyway, and if what's going to happen
Will happen anyway, then what's the use—
But if I'd known—

R. P. W.:   Well, there you go again.
Back on the old track, the desperate circle.
"If I had known—" and once you say those words
You'll end by saying all those other words
You've said, and the great Machine of History
Will mesh its gears sweetly in that sweet **lubrication**
Of human regret, and the irreversible
Dialectic will proceed. That is, unless—
"If I had known"—that is, unless we get
Some new and better definition of *knowing*.

ISHAM: Well, knowing—hell, it's just to know **a thing**,
Like anything you know—

R. P. W.:   No, knowing is,
Maybe, a kind of being, and if you know,

Can really know, a thing in all its fullness,
Then you are different, and if you are different,
Then everything is different, somehow, too.

Oh, well, this won't help now, even if there's some
Blind fumbling toward sense in what I say.
It won't help you, or that scared black boy George,
Or anybody else in the meat-house there.
The fire cracked high and made the chimney hum,
And light and shadow danced and swung together,
And your hands were sweating on the pistol butts,
And the people scrouged and hunkered by the wall
And watched your face, and you felt your own mouth moving
But couldn't hear the words. And then the door—

ISHAM: The door swung open. It was George fell in.
On knees and elbows, like he'd had a shove.
But hadn't had a shove. He just fell in.
Like somebody running and he barely makes it
To get home safe and fall inside the door,
Or like somebody when he swims too far
And suck or chute nigh gets him, and the sky
Swings high and black to make his eyeballs bulge.
But he makes it in. Then falls down on the ground.
That nigger was like that. He just fell down.
He held the pitcher handle in his hand.
But the pitcher was gone. The pitcher wasn't there.

R. P. W.: Did that surprise you?

ISHAM: No, so natural-like,
Like it had happened some long time ago.

R. P. W.: And George himself felt it, no doubt, as some
Peculiar fulfillment he had long lived with.

ISHAM: "Get in!" the voice said from the dark outside.
I saw that face that swung out there in the dark.
'Twas like a face that came from dark and air,
And it was Lilburn's face. It said: "Get in!"

So George crawled in. Lil shut the door, and stood.
"Now tie him up," For that was what Lil said.
Nobody moved. Not me, and not a nigger.
Lil said: "I give you niggers exactly a minute
To get that bastard tied." Two came and tied him.
George squinched his eyes tight, laying nigger-mum.
Lil stepped across him, like he wasn't there.

There was the block, four feet across, or nigh.
Nice tulip-wood, it was a whopping tree,
A section-cross, and smooth to lay your hand.
Lil slapped his hand down: "Put the bastard here."
They did it. And durn, the funny thing was this,
How that fool nigger sort of curled up there,

Drew up his knees to make himself all little,
To lie all on that hunk of tulip-wood
And not hang over, and be little there,
A-lying sidewise, and his eyes squinched shut.

I reckon that fool nigger sort of figured
That what you never saw just wasn't real,
So squinched his eyes. I reckon he found out.
Maybe he squinched his ears up too, and never
Even heard what Lilburn said when Lilburn said,
"Hand me that meat-axe, Ishey." And I did.

The people moaned and hunkered to the wall.
And maybe that fool nigger never heard
What Lil said then about the spoons and cups
And how they lost and broke 'em just for spite,
And tore the sheets where my mother lay and died.
And never heard him say: "But now's the last
Black son-of-a-bitching hand to ever,
So help me God, to make my mother grieve!"
The axe came down. Lil flung the hands in the fire.

R. P. W.: Enough. We know the rest—

ISHAM: And yeah, the
                                 axe came down,
And whacked his feet because they ran away.

Lil whacked 'em off and flung 'em in the fire.
And the axe—

R. P. W.:   Enough, we know the whole preposterous
Butchery, and Lilburn's mouthings, and the black folks'

moans—

But one thing more: Did George cry out at last?

ISHAM: Yeah, that fool nigger spread his mouth to yell.
You got to yell when they start chopping you.
He must of yelled, but I ne'er heard a sound,
Like all that nigger yelled was just a hunk
Of silence—you don't even hear it when the meat-axe
Gets in, gets through, goes *chunk*, and chunks on wood.
It's funny how that *chunk* just won't come clear.
Yeah, in my head, and I see the axe come down,
And not a sound, and that nigger spreads his mouth,
And not a sound, and I just strain and strive
To plain hear something—and Lord, if I only could—
For if I hear it, then maybe something's finished.
And it's not real, and yet I know it's real—

JEFFERSON: Oh, it is real. It is the only real thing.
Pain. So let us name the truth, like men.
We are born to joy that joy may become pain.
We are born to hope that hope may become pain.
We are born to love that love may become pain.

We are born to pain that pain may become more
Pain, and from that inexhaustible superflux
We may give others pain as our prime definition—

ISHAM: I just can't hear it when that axe comes down.
Looks like I'd hear it if it's really real.
And when that nigger spreads his mouth all wide—

JEFFERSON: Oh, I'm not talking now about that boy
Hacked to his death, and his scream in the midnight
                                        meat-house.
For what's one nigger more in the economy of pain?
Or talking about my kinsman Lilburn now,
For what's one more bloody and sentimental maniac?
Or talking about you, Isham, trapped and stupid,
For what's one more corruptible simpleton?
Or talking about those people hunched by the wall—
Oh, yes, they moaned, but don't forget they tied him.
But what's one more example of cowardly connivance?

I am talking about the terrible texture in which
One episode of anguish evokes all anguish
And sets nerves screaming, and the white tendrils curl,
In black peripheries beyond the last stars.
I am talking about the circumstantial texture in which
The death of that black boy was the death
Of all my hope and—

R. P. W.:   If I am informed of the facts,
Though you could not, apparently, bring yourself to speak
Of the family scandal, you nevertheless declared,
In general terms of course, your abiding faith
In your old definition of man, and made the last boast
To be cut in stone, on your mountain in Albemarle,
To sum your life.

JEFFERSON: It is hard, when old, to surrender
What you have taken to be the significance of life.
My hope died hard, and I must be frank to confess
That at the moment of the first information
There was merely the shock, for I had not yet surmised
How hope but feeds on hope, and in the cat's cradle
We weave and call our life and philosophy,
There's the single strand that, if plucked—and in the
                                             card-castle
If we strike one card—no, it wasn't like that.
No, despite the violence of the first shock
At the news from Kentucky, there was no immediate
                                             impairment
Of the general structure of my human hope.
There was no preliminary shudder, and I said,
This is merely a personal anguish, and individual evil.

R. P. W.: But why, indeed, was there such personal anguish?
Lilburn was kin, that's true, but a grown man now,

Not now what you once had called the sweet parcel of flesh

on a pillow.

Blood thins with age and distance. So your anguish seems,
To me at least, excessive.

JEFFERSON: Excessive, perhaps.
But by what standard, excessive? I had no son.
Yes, Meriwether had been a sort of son.
He took my words and heeded, and I saw in him
An image of the straight-backed and level-eyed men who

would come

And be worthy of the gleaming miles of our distance.
But he was dead. Courage had failed him. Dead,
They told me, by his own hand, in Tennessee.
I thought of that desperate dawn, his pain, and I wept.
But there were my sister's sons, the dear sister
Who lived, somehow, all the years in my inward imagination,
And I had thought of her, gentle by cradle and hearthside,
And felt a pang of sweetness at what had long been denied me.
I controlled the heart-pang. There was always contrivance,

and the large hope.

And then she died, by the sad western river.
But left her sons. I had no son, but I said,
Her sons, far away, by the swale or inimical forest,
Will fulfill her, and her best hope, and my heart.
You know the rest, what happened. That was that.

But I could not accept it. I felt the intense pain.
Excessive, perhaps, to the occasion. I could not name it.
I said, it is age, and in age each human distortion defines us,
And the slow dynastic dwindling of blood would leave us
Alone at the night-edge. So now is the time, I said,
To buckle the heart past fond accident, or failure,
And know that my hope lies in the general human fulfillment.

But the pain persisted, and the encroachment of horror.
I saw the smile of friendship as a grimace of calculation.
I saw the victuals on my plate in their undeclared context,
Mucous of oyster, beard of mussel, harslet of hog,
And even the choice viand as a shadow of ordure.
My eyes would wander from the instructive page,
And my heart crunched like a chick in the sow's jaw.
I said, I must cling more sternly to the rational hope.

But the axe had been laid, in secret, at the root of hope.
There had been severance of the secret vein,
And of the delicate conduits and commitments
Of being, and as History divulged
Itself, I saw how the episode in the meat-house
Would bloom in Time, and blooms in all characteristic
Episodes, and blooms in the lash-bite,
And blooms in the lost child's cry
Down in the quarters when the mother is sold.
Oh, yes, I've heard it, but I know, too,

How vanity and blood-lust may link obscenely
In the excuse of moral ardor, and a cause,
And the Christian Cherokee could readily tell you
How the heart bled westward on the Trail of Tears—

R. P. W.: Well, speaking of Indians, the Smithland courthouse
Has one nice record, how one Saturday night
In Eddyville, down in a tavern there,
Some heroes of our national destiny
Kicked an old Chickasaw, Jim, to death, for sport.
And as for Negroes, George is not alone.
An inquest tells how one man with a club,
On horseback, in the woods—

JEFFERSON: Oh, it's always the same.
Always the same, and the dust always drinks blood,
And Bloody Angle and the Bloody Pond—
Listen, flames crackle through the Wilderness
And the green briar burning smells like myrrh, but that other
More pungent odor is not myrrh, the odor
That so reminds you of the odor in the meat-house.
The wounded scream. Then cease. The flame has found them.

Well, let them scream. All's one in the common collusion.
Yes, the sarcasm is trivial, but if sarcasm
Is the only means left to detach oneself from that
Common collusion, I'll be sarcastic and remember

A few more items from the ample documentation,
And Pittsburgh and Pinkerton and the Polak bleeding
In some blind angle while the snow falls slow,
And Haymarket, and Detroit, and Henry's goons,
And high engirt in whiskered smuggery
I recall a certain broad-browed scholar, the pride of
                                    Harvard, who made
Good learning pimp for brokers, and he became
The common hangman, and the Dagoes died,
And Boston slept, and Philadelphia, too,
And sleep was easy over the great continent,
It was easy over the starlit continent I once had loved,
For all was safe now, and the stars held their
Accustomed formations. Take your screw. And sleep.
If you can sleep. If you can sleep. If you
Can no longer hear now the scream from the meat-house.

ISHAM: It looks like I just can't hear that nigger.
That nigger spreads his mouth, but I swear to God
I can't hear nothing—

JEFFERSON: Well, you're lucky then.
If you can't hear him scream, then you can sleep.

ISHAM: But that's the trouble, looks like could I just
One time just hear that yell, then I could sleep.
But I just can't.

JEFFERSON: Oh, what's one nigger dead,
One nigger more or less—except he's all,
And all responsibility now spreads.
It spreads like a stain in water, and—

R. P. W.:   Well,
If you would speak of responsibility,
There's the not unfashionable notion to consider
That George himself was quite responsible.

JEFFERSON: Oh, yes, he broke the pitcher—a miserable
                                                        pitcher.

R. P. W.: Only because he wanted, in the end,
To curl on the meat-block, draw his knees up little,
And squinch his eyes and know the expectant deliciousness
Before the axe fell—oh, yes, you have seen the wheat
When the reapers ring round the last of the standing grain,
How the rabbit runs to the stone hurled by the boy's hand,
And the stone's parabola and the rabbit's irrational
Skitter fulfill each other, and that fulfillment is a chord
Of music, enormous, to blacken the sky,
And the hen in the dark hen house offers her throat
To the delicate stitch of the weasel's tooth and to the lip's
Insidious suction, and with one muted squawk, automatic,
                                                        surrenders
To that saccharine surgery—and with the prurience of morning
You've seen in the hen house the blowsy victim askew,

Like an over-nourished matron on the divan,
Out-thrust and disordered, the eyes yet closed, hands lax,
After the hired lover has taken his exit.

JEFFERSON: So you'd make pain the final obscenity?
And after that obscenity nothing—nothing—

R. P. W.: No, don't blame me, I just report a notion.
But just suppose it true, what then? The victim
Becomes the essential accomplice, *provocateur*—
No, more, is the principal—and the real victim
Is he whose hand was elected to give the stroke,
But is innocent. So the line of the old poem,
See where the Victor-victim bleeds takes on
A new significance, and the Victim is Victor,
Not because, as the poem so quaintly affirms,
The just deed will blossom from the dust
And the lover of justice, though Victim, be vindicated,
But because the Victim is lover of injustice—
That is, of sweet injustice to himself.
And George trembles with sweetness at Lilburn's gaze,
Feels the lash already in that irreconcilable
And supplicating regard, comes back from the woods,
Not driven by hunger or fear, but drawn sweetly
Back to wreak his merciless frailty on Lilburn.
He comes back to curl on the meat-block and devise

A triumph like a trumpet, loud as blood.
Poor Lilburn, how could he escape, how—

JEFFERSON: Stop!
If there is truth in what you say—and yes,
There's truth, but a truth the heel would slew in
As it slews in ordure in the dark alley—
If, as I said, there's truth, it's still a truth
That extenuates nothing, and for you to make
Lilburn the victim is—

R. P. W.:   Oh, that's not it.
I only nag the question. And if Lilburn
Is George's victim, it's only a manner of speaking,
A way to say we're all each other's victim.
Potentially, at least.

JEFFERSON: What does that prove?
What does anything prove in the face of the naked scream?
What does anything prove in the face of—

R. P. W.:   Nothing.
Nothing, for there's no gold the acid of anguish
Will not, in the end, eat. And the axe fell.
And fell again. And when there was no sound,
Shall we suppose, but Lilburn's labored breath,
What remained on the block was heaved into the fire,
And the hot coals hissed, flame sagged, went blue and white,

Then settled dutifully to the new task,
And to the sound of that protracted sizzle
The prayers resumed by the wall. When all had burned—
That is, all that would burn—Lilburn said—

ISHAM: He turned round from the fire, and the people

hunkered,

And his face a-shining where the sweat had popped.
And quiet, just said: "You niggers stop that racket.
Or if you got to pray, you better pray
Dear God will help keep count on my mother's spoons,
And you won't break cups, nor tear a sheet she lay on.
Or you'll get fried before your mouth stops yelling.
You've seen that nigger George. Well, now you know."
And laughed right short. And said: "And by the way,
If anybody feels like telling tales
About what came to George, he might start thinking
How it would feel to fart your last sweet fart
On a bed of hot coals because your guts
Had just come to a nice boil inside you.
I mean what I say. And no man ever said
That Lilburn Lewis put his talk out cheap.
Now git!"

They get up quiet, and soft-foot long the wall.

He turned again, like something he'd forgot.
He called two back. They came. They stood and sweated.

"Get those damned bones," he said, "and dig a hole."
They dragged the bones. They put 'em in a bucket.
And we went out and watched the niggers dig.
No big hole, 'twas. They dumped the durn bones in.
The niggers left. And Lil, he stomped and smoothed
The ground all easy where the bones lay hid.

Then sudden-like I thought how quiet it was.
It was bright moonlight coming clear for frost.
"It's coming frost," I said, like nothing happened.
It felt so sweet and natural-like to say
How frost was coming, for the moon was bright.
It felt so natural, tears came in my eyes.
It felt so natural, like I loved the world,
And trees and rocks and stars and everything,
But now I feel a fool, a plain durn fool, for saying
How it looked like things all leaned and loved me, too.
And then—but then—

R. P. W.:   But then, no doubt, the earthquake?

ISHAM: Yeah, yeah, but I had just raised up my eyes
To see the moon, and my heart all big and sweet,
And then it hit. I fell down on the ground.

R. P. W.: Well, the folk version says you moaned and prayed
And called on God for mercy on your soul,

But Lilburn danced on the ground that shook like jelly
And cackled to the moon, and laughed at you,
And said: "What makes you call on God, you fool?
Don't call on God, He'd spit you in the face.
Call on the Devil, for he loves us both!"
And danced and cackled while the earth shook sick.

ISHAM: Oh, no—oh, no, it didn't come like that.

R. P. W.: I never thought it had. You see, that version
Would violate Lilburn's deepest character.
We know that Lilburn's not the Devil's son,
Even if the warrant that they swore for him
Does say in its old-fashioned formula
That Lilburn Lewis, named a gentleman,
Not having fear of God before his eyes,
But being moved and seduced by the instigation
Of the Devil, thus did his so-and-so and such.
No, Lilburn had no truck with the Evil One,
But knew that all he did was done for good,
For his mother and the sweetness of the heart,
And that's the instructive fact of history,
That evil's done for good, and in good's name—

JEFFERSON: But is not ever the less evil therefor,
Or for whatever mask or smirk may be devised,
And if evil is all—

R. P. W.:   Who said it was? I didn't.
For we might say that Lilburn's heart-deep need
To name his evil good is the final evidence
For the existence of good.

JEFFERSON: And if that's all,
Why not say evil is evil, and not sweeten
Your slobber with any pap of paradox?

R. P. W.: I think I know how trivial you find
My present argument, for I remember
How trivial I've found it now and then
In the face of brute facts. But anyway,
When the earth shook and oak trees moaned like men,
And the river sloshed like dish-suds and spilled out,
Poor Lilburn didn't name the Devil's name.

ISHAM: He fell down too, like me. I lay on the ground.
I lay and all my belly churned to die.
A noise came like a terrible wind to blow.
I saw the moon spin round, and the light get green.
I knew the End of Time. But I ne'er prayed.

And I lay there, and it came to me so awful
How a minute back I saw the moon all clear
And named it frost, how natural-like and sweet.—
But earth shook and threw me down. But I ne'er prayed.

What's there to pray for if the sweet thing came
So late and slow, and goes and leaves you lay?
Why don't it come a time when it can stay?
Why don't it come before the awful happened?
Oh, if things came, and time was easy time,
And the sweet time came, and night was common-still⌐
But, no—and durn, I wish I'd died and never
Knew how the sweet gets in your heart and swells
Till you think sudden: "Now—oh, now, it's different!"
But then it's not. Earth shakes, and throws you down.

R. P. W.: But you got up, for things don't end that easy.
And if God shook the country like a rug,
And sloshed the Mississippi, for a kind of warning—
Yes, that's the folk-say too, like Lilburn's caper.
Well, if God did it, why should God just pick out
Poor George as His excuse? There'd been God's plenty
Of such excuses, and they multiply
Right now in Old Kaintuck, but no earthquakes
In quite a spell, and no other Year of Wonders
To scare the home folks with the omens dread,
As when, night-long, the statue of Hercules,
In the Forum, sweated, and Commodus ate dung.

No, what great moral order we may posit
For old Kentucky, or the world at large,
Will scarcely account for geodetic shifts.

There was an earthquake, sure. But it just came,
And, Isham, threw you down. But you got up.
Got up, and lived, somehow.

ISHAM: The way folks live.
A thing will happen but you keep on living,
And every breath you draw or gobbet chewed
Just goes to say that nothing happened ever.

R. P. W.: Yes, we might say that life is possible
Only because of the discontinuity
Of life. You don't too often have to face
Life in a lump, your fate or definition.
So Isham lives, and sits with Lilburn still.
The mother's dead. The father's in Virginia.
Young George is hacked and burned and buried now.
Laetitia's gone—Aunt Cat got her away
With the midnight scream yet filling up her head.

LAETITIA: It filled my head, but I hung on the horse,

                                        and rode.

I made the settlement. They took me down.
They laid me on a bed, like I was little
And they would love me, for my name was Tishy.
But I knew there wasn't any love anywhere in the world,
Not now, not now—and when I tried to explain things,
The words, they came all wrong and—

BROTHER: They damn well did.

You gabbled like a guinea hen, and it was a skunk
Sucking her clutch of eggs. You lay and gabbled,
And never told me nothing, how he 'bused you.
You kept it from me, how I had a ground
To cut that bastard's heart out, like I would.
Yeah, you—you, Tishy, you made me out a fool,
And so when I rode up to Rocky Hill,
Why, he just named me "Brother," sweet as pie,
Said you were sick, like everybody knew,
And had your spells uneasy in your head.
He called that nigger, the one that's named Aunt Cat—
I never liked her, just too God-damn sly.
Says, "Yassuh, yassuh," while she bows and bobs,
And got a head-rag all too white and starchy,
And her too clean to be a nigger, too,
And peeking at you secret the whole time
Like you'd done dirty and she found it out.
Well, she came in. That bastard Lilburn called her.
He said: "Now name it how Miss Tishy left."
She bowed and scraped and made her head-rag bobble,
Then said it was the earthquake come and scared you.
Said you got notions how somebody yelled
Like he was hurt and killed and scared to die.
Then Lilburn stopped her: "Cat, did you hear something?"
So she looked slow at him and squinched her eyes:
"Now what you ast me, Mr. Lil, my Honey?"

Said it so sly you want to cut her throat,
And ain't no nigger gonna call me Honey.

Then Lilburn told her: "You better listen better.
I said, did you hear yelling here last night?"
"Why, Chile," she said, and squinched her eyes up sly,
"Whatever 'twas I heared, you heared it, too."
"Damn it," says Lilburn, "you try and recollect,
And tell the gentleman how poor Miss Tishy
Gets things mixed up. Now you—did you hear something?"
Then Cat says: "Lawd!—oh, Lawd I hears it yit,
Hit fills my ears, so turble wild hit comes,
And keeps a-comin, and hit comes and comes—"
"God-damn," says Lilburn, and his face went dark.
And I said: "Lilburn, I'd just like to know
Whatever the hell it was your nigger did hear."

"The owl," she said, "he scritch. And scritch again."
And me, I said: "Now who the hell cares
If a scritch owl scritches? Let the bastard scritch."
"He scritch agin," she said, "and then hit come!"

"What came?" said Lilburn, sharp. He grabbed her arm.

"Honey," she said, all gentle-like, and sly,
"Why, Honey, nothin. Jist the ole yearth-quake."

R. P. W.: So Cat now tortured Lilburn for her sport,
Just teetered on the verge of dire revelation,
Then caught her balance: "Jist the old yearth-quake."
It must have been a sinister sport for Lilburn.
No, not a sport. She didn't mean it that.
Rather, another show of doubleness.
She would set the scene for poor Laetitia's tale,
Not tell it herself, for Lilburn was her Honey—
Deny Laetitia's tale, but in denial
Declare the truth and proclaim the secret of the bestial hour.

BROTHER: She didn't pro-claim nothing, that fool nigger.
Just named the earthquake, then she squinched, and said:
"Ain't nothin happened here at Rocky Hill.
Not here at Rocky Hill. We loves each other."
And Lilburn said: "Get out." And out she got.

He looked round then at me, and said, "Dear Brother,
You've heard the nigger tell what happened here.
A chimney fell, the river roared—that's all.
It scared your sister, my beloved wife,
But when she's ready to come back, you tell her
The door is open, and my arms are open, too,
And my heart will break with her society gone."
He talked so fine, just like he was a preacher,
And shook my hand, and slapped me on the shoulder,

And poured me likker, and I drank it down.
And I rode off. By God, I just rode off.
Yeah, you—you, Tishy—you made a fool of me.

R. P. W.: But it was her gabble got the gossip started
About grim goings on at Rocky Hill,
And sent the Sheriff.

                    It's half a social call,
The country bumpkin somewhat overawed
By Lewis greatness and old Tom Jefferson.
He says he's heard they had some nigger-trouble.
"Why, yes," says Lilburn. "It's that nigger George.
I had him beat. You know how niggers are,
You get one ornery, just one thing to do.
I did it, and he high-tailed for the woods."
And says: "And I hope he don't come back." And shrugs.
And that's impressive to the frontier Sheriff,
That shrug. Three hundred dollars run away
To the high timber, but a Lewis sits and shrugs.
He takes his dram. He goes. The slaves don't talk.

And life goes on at Rocky Hill, goes on
And enters a phase of stillness, enters the silence.
What's there to do or say? All's done. All's said.
And Lilburn's soul lolls in his breast, lapt
In a dark, luxurious satiety.

It stretches its kingly members in dark somnolent ease.
It is a beast, it is a god, its belly
Is distended with the fullness of that delicious ingurgitation.
And do we think of eyes that close,
And unclose, slow and with muted glitter in
That glutted indolence of dark?

And so they sit, night after night, the two,
Lilburn and Isham, ringed by the silence,
Ringed by the continent that breathes in darkness.
No cups are broken now. No spoons are lost.
No linen sheet is torn, where Mother lay.
The foot is set soft to the floor-board, the dish
Makes contact with the table, but no sound.
There is order in the house and all the appurtenances
Of civilization defended. Lilburn was right,
And the portraits stare from the wall, in approbation.
The house had been set on the headland, on stone, against
The disorder of the wild land. Lilburn defends it.
Lilburn would defend civilization and define
The human mission, bring light to the dark place.
But what does he defend? Only a pitcher,
As some poor symbol, not the truth itself.
He defends the letter while the spirit flees.
And how define the human? By love of Mother,
And in affirming love lifts high the meat-axe.
How bring the light? He does not bring the light.

He plunges his heart into the unredeemed dark of the
>> wild land.

Does Lilburn know all this? He does not know.

Lilburn and Isham sit by the fire and wait.
The winter wanes, Time is divulged, and the earth
Yet shakes by day, day after day, but with
Diminishing violence, and men come to accommodate
The heart to the horror. Why not? Long ago,
They had accommodated themselves to being men.
And the work of the world goes on, the axe-blade
Rings clear in the oak that is frost-bound like iron, the season
Comes on, there will be space for corn, in season.

The red-bud shall order forth its flame at the incitement
>> of sun.

The maple shall offer its golden wings for the incitement
>> of air.

Powder of oak-bloom shall prank golden the deerskin shirt
>> of the woodsman, like fable,

Gleaming and wind-tossed, the raw conclamation of crows
>> shall exult in March sun from the swale-edge,

And the ceremony of joy be validated in the night-cry.
But the walks of old pleasure are, to him, now desolate,
The path by the river and the inspiring point of
>> bluff-vantage.

And desolate are the accustomed provinces of pleasure,
Where the fish will leap without fear of his cunning,
And in the season when bark slips on the elm twig
And the wild turkey gabbles and the hunter looks to

                         unhouse himself,

Lilburn's face will not be seen in sun or striation of shadow.
The bee shall take cognizance of the first bloom,
And gold thighs, drowsy with pollen, drift, like sleep, in the

                         sunlight,

But the old fulfillments now seem vanity.
The hour of owl-hoot, or crepitation of cricket-cry,
Means nothing to him now, and fails to evoke
The melancholy tenderness of dear sentiment,
And the fox-bark in thicket, with its sneezing excitement,
Goes without notice. The rain-crow shall croak in vain.
His heart does not unlatch at the thought of the time when

                         the first shoots

Of corn shall prick punctiliously the black field.
He does not respond now to the insinuation of nature
Or to the delicate irony of its repetitions,
For he inhabits an inward landscape
Of forms fixed and hieratic, like moon-blasted basalt.

But Lilburn is gentle now with Little Ishey—
With that strong young brute that wears the gentle face.
And is gentle with the people of the house.

They watch him secret, cannot understand.
But he can be gentle now, because he knows
That the time draws on, and Time fulfills itself.

The hound now finds the bone, and it is spring.
The jawbone of poor George, tradition says,
And says that God had sent the earthquake especially
To throw the bones out—but, of course, also
As a general expression of Divine displeasure.
But dogs like bones, even fine Virginia hounds,
And dogs have dug a bone up, now and then,
Without involving Seraphim or earthquakes,
And had there been no hound or bone to help
We know that Lilburn could have found his fate,
For all the Lilburns of the dark world know
The inviolability of wind,
And they know
The terror of the mole's, and the earthworm's, way.
Know the endeavor of frost in stone.
They know it.
But it's the hound, the loved hound from Virginia,
That works poor Lilburn's deepest will, and betrays him.

By the trace, with the bone, the hound now crouches,

                                and waits,

While red-birds whistle and the flame wing weaves,
And all earth breathes its idiot and promiscuous
Promise: *joy*.

The man comes down the trace.

He sees the hound, and knows the bone as human.

He takes it to town. The Sheriff gets the bone.

It's human, fire-black, and some shred of flesh

Yet clings where flame or hound-tongue had failed in duty.

The bone is scarcely evidence, but we guess

How far the gossip's gone if this can make

The Sheriff jam his hat on, yell for his horse.

And we can guess how in the web of grievous

Suspicion sick Laetitia's gabble wove,

The Sheriff's own name threaded with the warp.

We hear the voices: "Yeah, the bastard's skeered."

The voices: "Yeah, he'd lick a Lewis' spit."

The voices: "Yeah, I bet he taken his'n."

He hears the voices, hears them in his head.

And so leaps up. By God, by God, he'll show 'em.

By God, he'll prove a Lewis ain't nothing.

To him, noways. He rides to Rocky Hill.

ISHAM: Yeah, there they come, him and his men a-riding,

And Lil, he watched, and in a whisper-like:

"The Sheriff, look!" I figured he was scared,

And turned to him, all sick that Lil was scared.

He wasn't scared. Not Lil. His eyes were shining.

"Well, gentlemen!" he called, all fair and hearty,

"Get down, I'm proud you've come." They get down slow.
Slow, and their looks all set scantwise. Lil said:
"And Sheriff, take a drink and honor me."
He hummed and hawed, the Sheriff. Then squared off:
"Well, Mr. Lewis, I'll say much obliged
For yore good likker, but I'm here for duty.
I'll pray you, sir, to call yore niggers up."
And Lil just smiled so cool: "Why, Sheriff, sure.
My house is yours, poor thing though it may be."
The Sheriff then: "They ain't a damn thing wrong
With yore big house. You take me fer a fool?"
And Lil, he steady smiled and said so soft:
"Why, Sheriff, that's a sort of way of talking
To be polite. For who might know it so."
"God-damn," the Sheriff said, and flushed up black.
He chewed his mad. Then quiet: "I want them niggers."
And Lil: "Why, Sheriff, sure. Now, Ishey, call 'em."

I got the niggers and they all stood there.
The Sheriff pulled a parcel out his pocket,
Wrapped in a rag, his handkerchief I guess.
He gave it to Lilburn. "Look at that," he said.
And Lil, he unwrapped it slow. It was a bone.
It was a jawbone, black where fire had burned.

"You know that bone?" I heard the Sheriff saying.
And Lilburn say: "A bone's a bone, and, Sheriff,

If you believe you have a duty here,
Then do it. And get gone. I've things to do
Than handle all the offal you drag in."
And dropped the bone.

                              The Sheriff picked it up.
And flushed for mad. He held it in his hand.
He swung to the niggers then and held it high:
'This is a nigger's bone, and you know who.
I am the Law, I say I want his bones.
Show me them bones. If you don't, by God, you'll be
A coward passel of niggers, like you are."
He stopped, and stood. And Lil, he stood and smiled.
The Sheriff waited, and nobody said.
And Lilburn smiled, and said: "You see." So soft.

If Lil said nothing, maybe till this day
Those niggers might just stood all sull and mum,
And never said, and bones been in the ground.
"You see," he said, "you named 'em what they are."
And laughed. "A passel of niggers." He turned, and spat.

And then it happened, came a voice so high
And old and screechy, like some old scritch owl,
But not a-night, and scritched to fill the air.
"Bones will fly up!" it scritched. "Them bones will rise.
I see them bones, they're flyin to the sky!"

And laughed a scritchy-cackle, crazy-wild.
It was Aunt Cat. She fell down on the ground.

But who did see, or give a care to see?
The niggers yelling so, and gabbling wild.
"Them bones!" they yelled, and some were crying, too,
And some were looking wild up in the sky,
And one—one of the blue-gums what had tied up **George**—
He ran to the Sheriff, and fell down on the ground,
And he was blubbering, that fool nigger, then—
"Oh, white folks, save me, and I'll show them bones!"

R. P. W.: So that was it. It was Aunt Cat again.
Not that she did it—she would not betray
Her Honey-Chile she once had given suck to.
No, not betray, but in her doubleness
Contrive the engine of betrayal, yet
Be completely guiltless. Oh, she would never tell,
Nor show the bones, but saw them in the sky.

But why right then? What made her seize that moment?
An easy guess: it was that Lilburn spat.
Long back, remember, when Miss Lucy died
And Cat reminded how she'd given suck
And was his Mammy too, then Lilburn spat.
Spat out her milk, and all her niggerness.
"A passel of niggers," now he said, and spat.
And thus has tripped the latch of the old anguish,

And nigger bones fly up and kiss the sky.
Oh, it's no trick, no subterfuge, for she sees
The bones fly up, avenging and redeemed,
And utters her screech of glory and anguish and then
Collapses. And knows the end, and knows her Honey-Chile,
Her Lil is gone. And so shuts tight her eyes.
She lies on the ground and lets the human confusion
Blow past, blow past like dust, like dead leaves whirled.
The white folks go. The black folks tote her in.

ISHAM: They dug the bones and put 'em in a sack
And hung the sack by the Sheriff's saddle-bow.
"Now Mister Lewis," the Sheriff up and said,
"If hit's yore pleasure, now I guess we'll ride."
"It is my pleasure, sir," Lil said, and laughed.
He laughed, and hummed some tune. So we rode off.

R. P. W.: Did he already have the end in mind?
Lilburn, I mean. No, I should reckon not.
Just had the certainty of moving toward
That perfect certainty of self that all
His life had leaned toward. The cliff trees,
Even in stillness, in the track of the old blast,
Lean, and will lean, with that prevailing and pitiless power.
And the compass knows the unpulsing flow in its steel.
The only knowledge worth the knowing is
The knowledge too deep for knowing. Let us lean

With the powerful formulation of the old blast.
And love the north, in darkness faithful.
For certainty is all. What other value may we seek?

So Lilburn took his certainty to town,
And found some guarantors to make his bond.
We know their names, a Rogers, Bolen, Dyer,
Cannon, and Hollinshead, their names, that's all,
And good names yet from the old time in Kentucky,
Good householders of that dark vicinage,
Good men of property, now dead and gone.
Five thousand dollars pledged. An empty gesture:
Lilburn could stand for that and multiply.
And so back home. Back home to wait.

                              To wait.

For what? Well, one old version has it,
They waited for the time of the Grand Jury
And hired a spy in town to bring the word,
Of what the Jury found, true bill or no.
True bill it was, the lathered rider said,
And so before the Sheriff came again
To rearrest and hale them back to town
They had the time to do what they would do.
The Sheriff came too late. He found it done.

But that account's not true. Too bad, it's tidy
To have the spy spur up with provocation,

And have the Sheriff hot behind, too late.
It's just too bad we're stuck with the documents.
We're stuck with fact, and the slow turn of time.
And here's the fact: On March 19 the Jury
Took evidence and didn't linger long.
True bill it was, and murder: *Lilburn Lewis,*
He, with an axe of the value of two dollars ($2.00)
Held in his hands, did willfully and maliciously
And with hate, cut a death wound—

And Time turns slow, and the orbed axis leans
To warm Kentucky closer to the sun,
To swell the corn-grain in the rank earth's dark
And sprig the black earth with the corn's bright blade
Among the black boles fire had left to rot.
But there is forest yet, and buds are bursting,
And morning's march wakes birdsong mile by mile,
First drowsy note in the green gloom, then the glory.
Song washes westward through the wilderness.
The dawn lifts westward, and the dogwood bursts.

This is the hour of Lilburn's sleep, the hour
When dream turns inward, groping for the heart.
His dream now finds the heart. Ah, all is easy.
It makes its mansion there. It takes its ease,
And that poor body sprawls on the tumbled bed.
In dawn, the swart face now is streaked with pale.

The lips are parted. Hush, the breath drags slow.
One arm is flung to the bed's emptiness,
And the faint odor of vomit would assail the nostrils.

Waking, he will, no doubt, be seized as ever
By a momentary incredulity,
And think: "But it's not me, oh, it's not me!"
Then know. But before the glacial acceptance, cry,
Cry out just once, to the empty room: "God!"
Then know, and be, himself. And the day's development
Will unfold, slow, its dear necessity.
Ah, man must love his own necessity,
But it is hard to find, so hard and slow.
The last phase: the threshold of recognition.
The last phase: the kiss of necessity.
The last phase: the self fades into fate.

So Lilburn waits. He waits in confidence.
He trembles on the threshold. Joy stirs.
Joy flickers, shy, in the heart's cold fatigue.
Yes, he is tired. But joy is energy.
There is one source of joy, and only one.
There is one germ for joy. Its name is vision.
The scales are loosed on his eyes. Its name is vision.
While vision grows, he sits with his younger brother,
By the cold hearth, and the April night grows big,

And darkness peers in through the open door,
And the annual fragance now, like memory, **swells**
In darkness to seduce the heavy sense,
And the peepers, far away, prick the night
With their insidious silver monotone,
And from some forest enclave spied by stars,
Some star-stung dingle where the deep woods hush,
The whippoorwill offers his heartbroken comment.
It comes here faint, but with veracity.
And if you were outside the house you'd see,
Below the bluff, by the forest's dark verge,
How the first fireflies are tremulous, and now try
To copy heaven with their humble stars,
And that frail illumination is sustained in the strong hand of
                                                    darkness,
And far below, the great river is steady in starlight.
You'd see these things if you were not inside,
With candle, jug, cold hearth.

ISHAM: Yeah, in the house.
We'd sit inside, the candle sagging low,
And Lil was writing like he did those nights,
His paper spread and the gray goose-quill by.
He'd lean and study on a thing to say,
Then write it down, all slow to make it fair,
Then lean and study. Then might tear it up.

One night I asked, and he just snapped short at me.
"Business," he said, "and business not for boys."

Then in the window, where the dark night was,
It came a-sudden, but like the stillest breath,
A big green moth, so big you'd never see,
The palest green like some ghost leaf alive,
So big, blown on a breeze you couldn't feel,
Nor brush your cheek with cool, but it was there.
Then that big moth, it came so ghost-green by,
And settled on the paper nigh to Lil.
Lil looked at it. He looked all steady-slow.
Then lifted up his hand, so steady and slow.
The moth, it moved its wings so quiet and slow,
And Lil kept staring at it waiting there.
Lil's hand rose up.

         I saw it waiting there.
The hand I mean, high in the air, and I knew
That if that hand came down like it could come
So heavy-strong and fast like a painter's paw
And did what it could do, then that would be
The end of something, but durn, I couldn't say
Just what. But just one second, sudden-cold,
I hated Lil. And that was terrible.
I saw the hand up high, and sort of sick

The hate came sudden and I sweated there.
I saw the hand. And then the hand came down.
But not to scare, and touched the table top.
And never stirred. And so my breath came back.

And then that green thing moved, but ne'er a wing.
It crept up slow. It clomb on Lilburn's finger.
The finger never moved. The thing climbed up.
And now the wings all gentle fanned, and slow,
But not to fly, but like it had a mind
To spread and make a show for folks to see,
And the wings moved pale there in the candlelight.
Then slow Lil's hand rose up, up high again.
So high Lil reached, then stopped. It didn't scare.
Not that, but slow it drifted off his hand.
The wings ne'er moved not much to fan and fly.
It drifted off just like the time had come
To go where it would go, and say good-bye.
And it was gone, and Lil just watched the air.
The thing was gone in the dark outside our door.

Lil's hand came down. He turned to me, and said:
"You asked me what I wrote, Old Ishey-Boy."
He sort of smiled. "Well, read it, here it is."
He shoved the paper at me, and I read.
In the Name of God Amen This my last will—

I saw the words, and all my guts went cold.
"Why, it's your will," I said. And he just grinned.
"You make your will," he said, "when the time draws on."
"But, Lil—" I said.

"And the time draws on," he said.

"But, Lil—" I said, and all my breath got choked
Like nights when the nightmare came and I'd wake up
And feel my throat, then know it was a dream.
"Oh, you're afraid they'll hang us," I heard him say.
And saying it, he named my dream. Then grinned:
"Well, Ishey-Boy, we sort of killed the nigger."
And me: "But just a nigger"—and my breath got choked—
"But just a nigger that done our mother wrong!"

He slapped my knee. "Forget it, son," he said,
"I'll never let 'em hang my Ishey-Boy."
Then sharp he said: "Read on." And didn't grin.
And I read on, and read about his business,
And how he left our father his fine horse,
The one he bought of Hurley, with the blaze,
And to our father, too, off in Virginia,
His rifle-gun, shot-bag, and walking stick,
For natural life, and the hound-dog Nero he loved so well.
And how he named Laetitia beloved but cruel.
And all his business. But the words looked queer,

And I kept on thinking how it wasn't true,
And nothing, nothing, ever had been true.
By God, it wasn't true. I threw it down.

He picked it up, and shoved it back at me.
"Read on," he said. And so I read the words:
Within this inclosure myself and brother requests
Be entered in the same coffin and
In the same ground. But *ground* scratched out, and then
'Twas *grave* he'd writ. I read the words, just words.
Then all a-sudden I saw the sense, and all.
Saw *brother* writ. And knew the word was me.
'Twas me, 'twas Isham, in the ground and grave.
And so called out: "But, Lil—it's me that's here!"
And he right soft: "Why, Ishey, yes, it's you."
"But, Lil," I said, "you just now said they wouldn't—"
"Oh, Ishey-Boy," he said, "oh, you can trust me."
"But, Lil," I said, "you lay me in the ground,
And in the grave, and—"

                    So then he leaned at me,
And said so soft: "Oh, Ishey, not alone."
"But dead!" I cried. And then he spat, and said:
"What's to be dead?" And jumped up from his chair:
"You can be dead and breathe and eat and sleep
And purge your gut and walk inside your clothes.
Oh, see the folks all walking in their clothes!

Don't know they're dead and stinking in their clothes!"
And he stared like folks was there, but I couldn't see 'em.

"But, Lil," I said, "but, Lil, it ain't us dead!—
For listen, listen, we can up and ride,
Get saddled up and gone and fast and far,
Tonight, and ride, and ride to Mississippi
Or down to what they name the Arkansas,
Or West like Cousin Meriwether went
To spy the land and where folks' foot would come,
Where mountains are big and where the ocean is—
Oh, it's a country wide and parlous big
And empty for the days and nights to come,
And safe to be, like 'twas a new world come—"

"The world," he said. And spat: "It's all the same!
Where'er you go, the world all stinks the same.
The day's the same, and night, or light or dark—"
And me: "But, Lil—but, Lil—we'd be alive!"
And his eyes went naked like he hated me,
And he said low: "Yes, you would ride away,
Just up and ride and leave our mother here."
"But, Lil, she's dead—" And him: "She loves you still.
But you don't love her, you would ride away,
For you're just scared they'll hang you with a rope."
He grabbed his neck, and let his tongue stick out
Like he was hanging. But a-sudden laughed, and said:

"Oh, Ishey, I'll not let them hang my boy.
They'll never string up Ishey like a cat,
Not my Old Ishey up to kick and squirm
And wet his pants while all the folks all laugh.
Oh, no!" And took a step to me, and leaned,
And talked so low, a voice to hardly hear.

But I could hear his voice: "There is a way.
For you are Isham. And I will show the way.
You're Ishey-Boy, and you will come with me.
You will be with me and Mother. There's a way."
And so he lower leaned, and said the way.

R. P. W.: So had you there, at last. Yes, all was his.
Now he could sit while dawn and day came on,
And take his ease, and all his soul be still.

ISHAM: Yeah, yeah, we sat till light came slow, and slow
The candle died before the day had come,
And at the window, slow, the sky got gray,
And gray came in the window and the door.
And it was light. The hound licked Lilburn's hand.
The hound went to the door and smelt the air.
And it was light.

I heard the niggers come.
They brought the breakfast and they set it down.

Lil thanked 'em kindly. I ne'er touched a thing.
"Now, son," Lil said, "what's wrong with these good vittles?
Good hominy and ham and good red gravy?"
"Ain't nothing wrong," I said. And him: "Then eat!"
So he got up and slapped me on my shoulder,
And said: "Oh, Ishey-Boy, it is today.
Oh, Ishey-Boy, we go a journey soon.
But you can't start your travels when your gut
Will growl for empty. Come on, eat it up!"

I put some gobbets in my mouth, and chewed.
Then it was over, and the bright day came.
Lil up and put his papers in his pocket
That they would be there when the time came on.
We went outside to do what he had said.

R. P. W.: To face each other over your mother's grave?
That's what the record says, and by your word,
To stand and each present to the other's breast
The muzzle of the weapon and to wait
For the count to come.

ISHAM: Yeah, Lil would count to ten.

R. P. W.: Why not count three?—No, that would be too quick!
Lil couldn't watch you then, and relish all
That all his time had groaned for, hour by hour.

ISHAM: But what—what made him count so slow, and stare?

R. P. W.: To get the last sweet drop. But tough luck, Lil!
Right at the pay-off, the big moment now,
Just as you face each other at the grave,
You shoot yourself by accident, and so
The curtain's down before the show begins.
The tiddy's tough, all right—

ISHAM: But listen here—

R. P. W.: Listen to what?

ISHAM: To how it was.

R. P. W.:   What was?

ISHAM: To how it came. It never came like that.

R. P. W.: Why not? When they had caught you, brought

                                                                   you in,

On April 11, and John Darrah called
His jury up, he being Coroner,
You made your deposition and you swore
That *Lilbourne in trying an experiment*
Accidentally shot himself dead—
And they believed you, for the charge to you

Reads not for murder, just accessory
To Lilburn's death—

ISHAM: Yeah, but it wasn't true.

R. P. W.: Well, if you didn't swear the truth, then what?

ISHAM: Lil stood up there and started counting, slow,
And he stared steady at me all the time.
It looked to me I didn't know his face.
It looked to me like it was not my brother
To stare and count—count *four,* count *five,* count *six*—
No, not Big Bubber. No, it wasn't him.

R. P. W.: Well, what a fool I've been! I see it all.
How Lilburn counted slow to make you do it,
To strike him down, and be his last betrayer,
And leave him in that perfectest delight,
Alone, alone, in that sweet alienation
Wrapped in all wrong and the sweet injustice done him.
And don't you see how, as a corollary,
Because you loved him he betrayed you, too?
He betrayed you when he made you murder him,
He withheld the slug that would have set you free,
And broke his promise and his solemn word—
"Oh, Ishey-Boy, I'll never let you hang!"—

ISHAM: I could a-shot myself—I could a-done it—

R. P. W.: But Lilburn knew you never would. He knew you,
And knew you'd break and run, and just like George,
Take out for the woods. And he knew they'd dog you down.
Don't you know that?

ISHAM: I don't know nothing—nothing—

R. P. W.: You knew enough to shoot him, and enough
To swear the lie—oh, I don't blame you, mind—
To save your neck.

ISHAM: But that—but that's not why.
To live or die, by then I didn't care.
I knew they'd name me guilty anyhow.
But not like that, I didn't want folks saying
'Twas me killed Lilburn when he was my brother.
I couldn't tell 'em how it was, how sudden
It came, and how—oh, folks don't ever know
How things can happen, and they come so sly—
My gun went off. That's it. I didn't hate him.
It's just the gun went off. The slug went in.

I see the place, how blood came out so slow,
And Lilburn looking at me strong and strange.
And he just stands there steady like forever,
And I just hear that son-of-a-bitch of a bird,
In the woods, far off, and he just won't stop singing,

And Lilburn stares, and maybe if I listen
To that son-of-a-bitch of a bird just hard enough,
Then nothing happened, nothing, and Lil won't fall,
And everything will be just like it's not.

But Lil falls down. He just falls down. It's awful
To kill your brother like you hated him—

   R. P. W.: Well, why not now admit you hated him?
Why not? He'd brought you to the bitter pass.
Why not?

   LUCY: I do not know that I can say
Why not. But, Isham—oh, my son—I know
That you must not. For if you loved him once—

   JEFFERSON: Yes, you loved him once—and the more fool!

   LUCY: —for if you loved him truly, truly, once,
That love is valid yet, and is all you have.
It is all you can bring with you to the inhabited silence.
For if love's anything, it is the thing
That, once existing, may not be denied,
For it is definition, and denial
Is death, but is
That death in which you may not ever lie down.
So how could you, my Isham, ever hate him,

Even if your pain, that terrible morning, seemed like hate?
Or how could I myself have hated him,
Or even blamed him, knowing all wickedness
In its own pain will wash all guilt away?
And though, Isham, I had once, in weakness, failed my

obligation,

And had refused my obligation, and so died,
God was now good, and granted me the final fulfillment,
And I was prepared to accept my son Lilburn
That moment when he bore his burden forth
And stood above my grave, and the bullet came.

JEFFERSON: I would have fired it with my own hand!

R. P. W.: But look! Who's this?

JEFFERSON: Yes, who are you?

R. P. W.:   The eyes
Are black and staring, but the forehead, look!
It's broken, the brain stares out.

JEFFERSON: Well, Crack-head, who

are you?

MERIWETHER: Yes, I am Crack-head, but if I'm

Crack-head now,
You ought to recognize your handiwork.

JEFFERSON: My handiwork!

MERIWETHER: I am the man you did give the bullet to.
I am the man you killed. You knew my name.
I was your near-son once. You knew my name.
I was the one—

JEFFERSON: Oh, Meriwether, you?

MERIWETHER: Yes, Meriwether—

JEFFERSON: My son, I see the old mark of your pain,
But I cannot understand your charge, for I never,
In form or fashion whatsoever, contrived
But for your good, as far as I understood it.
By my poor will, I mean. And what miscarriage
Came toward that desperate dawn in Tennessee
When you groped the gourd in the dry bucket,
And the sad moon sagged westward and nobody came,
And you called for water, water, and nobody came—
It's not my doing, no! And I wept to hear.
You'll not say I—

MERIWETHER: I'll say the truth, for if
I lived a lie, and lived the lie you taught me,
I died a truth. I cracked my head and let
The lie fly wide—look! It's gone, there's nothing.

Look in the hole. Just the bloody pulp that is truth.
You see the gap. You made it—

JEFFERSON: Meriwether!

MERIWETHER: Yes, Meriwether, murdered by your lie.
It was your lie that sent me forth, in hope.
To the wilderness—

JEFFERSON: If it was ease you sought—

MERIWETHER: Don't be a fool. You know why I went forth.
Went forth and with your letter in my pocket,
The letter writ the Day of Liberty,
July 4, 1803. It said:
And to give more entire satisfaction & confidence
To those who may be disposed to aid you,
I Thomas Jefferson, President
Of the United States of America, have written
This letter of general credit for you
With my own hand and signed it with my name.
  TH: Jefferson.
                    But that could not save me.
Not from the lie. Nor later. So went forth.

I and my dear friend Clark, and forty-three men—
Soldiers, French watermen, the tough Kentuckians,

And my good nigger York, who left his seed
In every tribe across the continent—
And bales of junk to please the savages,
Breechclouts and scarlet cloth and burning glasses,
Red leggings, blankets, medals and ear-wire.
And so set forth, the month was May, we set sail
In the late afternoon breeze, camped on the first island.
And so entered upon my life. And my death.

Entered the land where the sky lifts west, like wings.
We entered the land of the enormousness of air.
For a year we moved toward the land of the Shining

                                     Mountains.
That is their name. It is their name all day in the long light.
We had long left the land of the honeybee.
Not since the Osage, but flowers sweet in the season proper,
And the bee-martin comes. This we could not understand.
There was much not easy to understand, the mountains
To the right hand, the north, and west of us, boomed like

                                           a bell,
One great stroke, lonely, or then more, and rapid
Like discharge of ordnance, six-pounders, the battery

                                           well timed.
The Minnetarees had told us of it. We thought they lied.
But we have heard the noise and do not pretend to

                                        understanding.
It is for philosophy to say. We were soldiers,

And simple. But recorded all days, the little event, and

the large.

As when we slew a wolf: *This day a yellow wolf was slain.*
The winter broke: *The sugar maple runs freely; swans pass*

from the north.

May came again: *The geese have their young, the elk begin*

to produce their young,

The antelope and deer as yet have not, the small species
Of whippoorwill begins to cry. We have scarce any thunder.
The clouds are generally white and accompanied with

wind only.

We moved across the land. We endured.
And after endurance, the snarl of mutiny. I flogged him.
He screamed at the dawn-stripes. The Indian, watching, wept.
And I would have wept in my heart, for I knew him,
And knew him to be only another of us, in the long travel.

And we suffered the rigor of seasons, white dew and

sun-heat, and the time

When the hibernants are withdrawn to the only comfort
In the iron world. And the snow on the far peak glared blue
In excess of light, and no track of beast on the unruffled
White of the high plain, no wing-flash in high air,
And in that glittering silence of the continent
I heard my heart beating distinctly, and I said,
Is this delight? Is this the name of delight?

We bore the exigency of flesh.

Tumors on legs, and flux. Boils and impostumes. Some
spat blood.

And diseases of foulness from clipping the female savage.

The savages make a brew of lobelia and sumac, the roots.

We tried it to soften the *lues*. Of use but not sovereign.

We saw and described the new beasts. We slew the great bear,

The horrible one, gray-grizzle and does not forgive.

Men see his tracks on the sand bar and are afraid.

We noted his color and how his testicles are great and hang
strangely under his belly.

The heart is of great size, and death comes most tardy,
with anger.

We ate the flesh of dog, but rejoiced. We ate peculiar flesh.

So we went on, and I sat on the blanket with chiefs.

They drew with a stick in the dust the lay of the land west.

On white elk-hide Twisted Hair drew me a map,

How the rivers converged west and sought the great lake of
the water ill tasted.

That is their name for the ocean. But none had been there.

This was the story of Twisted Hair. We came there.

We lay on our mats in the rain and heard the booming
of ocean,

But yet we had not seen it. Next day we saw.

And Clark, my friend, wrote in his papers thus:

O Ocian in view! O! the joy.

That was the cry of pride at simple achievement.

We had come a hard way, and that could not be gainsaid,

And pride in endurance is one pride that shall not be

                                    denied **men.**

O! the joy, Clark cried, but the inwardness of that joy

Of our long travel together was not yet revealed.

It was to be revealed upon our return

When the faces of my companions were withdrawn from

                                        my sight

And only imagination could speak truth of our common

                                        experience.

Truth? No: the last delusion. But that later.

Now was November. We wintered by that water,

And heard the great booming steady when storms strode.

It was a long way back, and returning we passed all the

                                        seasons.

Then St. Louis, and I broke the bread of civil men.

Of civil men! And would that I had stayed

And howled with savages and never returned here.

The bread of civil men—well, I had seen

The savage tear the steaming guts, and blood streak the

                                        cheekbone,

And would that I had wallowed and remained there,

And not returned. But did return, and discovered

That in the populous place of the civil contract

The civil breath breathes out the life. You had lied.

You had lied with persuasion to the need of my heart
And named me noble reasons for my utmost effort.
So I went forth. And returned. And then,
For one brief moment, my experience seemed confirmation
Of all you had said, and I had hoped for, for in
My imagination the voice remained of the night ocean
And the days of long travel together, and I thought that I
Now knew how men may travel long together
And move across land and time, and rejoice, for I
Was lulled in your great lie that men are capable
Of the brotherhood of justice.

          I became Governor.
Governor of all the West, headquarters St. Louis.
And the small lies gathered, too small to be seen. But they
                        hummed
Like midges over the mud-flats in the month of fever,
And treachery gleamed like green slime in the backwater.—
That Bates, whose hell-heart is a sink and bog
Of ordure—that Bates, he smiled. He stank in sunshine.
But Bates—he was but one of civil men.
And so I fled.

        Not westward as I should,
But east, and took my papers for my proof.
To Federal City—sure, in the capital
Where you had sat and writ and sent me forth,
There I'd find justice. So fled east for that,

Not guessing yet who the Great Betrayer was.

To Tennessee I came, at Chicksaw.
Drunk at Fort Pickering, not my custom.
I could not understand my own drunkenness.
Then in the wilderness found the Natchez Trace,
And fled. Fled my companions, fled their voices—
My Creole, my black boy, good Major Neeley.
I fled the human face and smile, and rode.
I rode toward Justice. I would kill the slander
That I'd embezzled and engrossed, that I—
I who had slept under the big stars—
Would peck at dollars as a sparrow at dung.
Yes, they said that. The very Government
Denied my drafts, refused my vouchers, sent
That paper back to plague me, and I paid.
Paid from my pocket. But lies grew. I fled.

Toward evening I came to the miserable inn.
Grinder's, the name. A work-sick woman with brats.
The husband away. Two huts in the wilderness.
The desperate corn-patch snagged with fire-black trees.
I asked for drink and took it, but not much.
I ate the food she gave me, but not much.
I could not understand my own agitation.
I sat outside the door and watched the evening
While peace came back then for a little space.
"It is a beautiful evening," I said to the woman.

I thought of the beauty of evening, moving west over the land.
Now in my cabin the woman spread my robes,
Bearskin and buffalo. I laid me down.
But not to sleep. To meditate on justice.
I rose and spoke aloud and declared myself.
In the disturbed darkness I declared myself.
For suddenly I knew there was no Justice.
No, not for me, nor any man, for the human
Heart will hate justice for its humanness.

Listen, had I but known the truth of the heart.
Had I not dreamed that good comes, even if not easy.
Had I not dreamed that man at last is man's friend
And will long travel together and rejoice in steadfastness.
Had I not loved, and lived, your lie, then I
Had not been sent unbuckled and unbraced
To find the end—oh, the wilderness was easy!—
But to find, in the end, the tracklessness of the human heart.

The discovery came late, and I was unprepared.
You had unprepared me. I hated you.
So seized the weapon primed and charged, and broke
In one blast the brain-pan, and flung the lie
Free to wing away, and let me sleep.

But could not die. And I cried out for water.
I crawled in the moonlight and groped the gourd in
                                        the bucket.

But the bucket was empty, and nobody came.
I could not die. I cried: "I am no coward,
No coward but so strong, and hard to die."
I remembered then how the great bear had died,
Tardy, with anger, under the plum trees. I knew him.
At dawn I died.

        I knew who murdered me.
I knew who flung my body into the hole
Where hog might come to root, or the wolf scrabble.
And after the turn of years some pedant fool
Had chopped his Latin for my garnishment
And chiseled up the lie I'd never have spoke.
I'd never say: "Oh, Good Republic, live!
And happier live my lost years in your own."
Oh, no. That Good Republic is of men,
So let them live their own years and not mine.
I solemnly curse them and the deeds of their hands.
No, do not flinch! I knew who murdered me.
And if you murdered me—

JEFFERSON: Not that, my son.

MERIWETHER: Yes, that. For in your lie was my death,
And if I learned anything in my earthly years,
It is that every lie is a death, for I died a death,
And especially that lie spoken in the vanity of virtue.

JEFFERSON: Vanity, no. It was but my hope that in the
exfoliation

Of years man might, in the end—

MERIWETHER: Yes, that sweet lie,
And I would honor more the axe in the meat-house,
As more honest at least, than your special lie
Concocted, though out of nobleness—oh, yes,
It was noble, but was concocted for your comfort
To prove yourself nobler in man's nobleness.
Yes, in man's nobleness, you'd be the noble Jefferson.
And if that is not vanity—

JEFFERSON: My son, be still a moment.
If what you call my lie was what undid you,
So be it, then. It has undone me, too.
For I, too, was unprepared for the nature of the world,
And unprepared, I confess, for my own nature,
And Truth, long since, began her hideous justice,
For all lies are avenged, at last, in the truth of pain.
But if there was vanity, was vanity, then, all?
By God, not all—

LUCY: And now, my brother, I see.
Yes, Meriwether's right. I begin to see.
I begin to see why your rejection of Lilburn—

JEFFERSON: Rejection, yes. Oh, you'd have me connive,
Like you, to pet the sentimental butcher.
Well, I'll accept no part of that responsibility.
If there's responsibility, it's yours,
And if it's yours—

LUCY: Yes, I must accept it,
The responsibility of my love, I mean, and—

JEFFERSON: And therefore,
You'd justify, and would have me connive to justify,
Your son's good work in the family meat-house?

LUCY: My dear brother, won't you understand what I mean?
Don't you understand that I, though I loved my son,
Would have seen him die in the direst pain, rather
Than know he had come to do the thing he did?

JEFFERSON: Then why blame my rejection?

LUCY: Yes, I blame
                                        you.
JEFFERSON: No, blame yourself. You bred him and you
                                        loved him.
LUCY: I told you, I accept the responsibility of my love,
And know, somehow, that my love was infected with failure.
No, I must maintain that my love in some part,

Some part at least, was love. Else how had I lived?
But even my love had infected my son's heart.
Oh, how can love—after all, dear God, it was love—
Be poison in even the first milk love would offer
To still the raw babe's wail in the world's dark?
What do I say? I do not know precisely—

JEFFERSON: But I know this, I'll have no part, no matter
What responsibility you yourself wish.

LUCY: I do not wish it. But how can I flee what is nearer
Than hands or feet, and more inward than my breath?
Yes, I tried once to flee responsibility.
I died. And my death was index of responsibility
Long since begun, for every fear and the fear—
Yes, that was it, it was the infection of my love—
All my dark fear of the dark, and the dark land.
No, not merely Kentucky—long before, it had begun,
And fear had been in the milk of my nipple, like fever,
And the babe took suck, and for that infected nourishment
                                        loved me—
JEFFERSON: And so chopped the nigger to defend your
                                        spoons!
LUCY: Was it for that? When my son had done the thing,
I could not understand. For spoons? For cups?
Because he loved me and would defend the vanities I'd loved?
Can you conceive the soft-foot nightmare of that question?
But now I say that what he would have defended

Was but himself against the darkness that was his.
He felt the dark from all the woods creep in.
He felt the dark fear hiding in his heart.
He saw the dark hand set the white dish down.
He felt the darkness growing in his heart.
He saw the dark faces staring, and they stared at him.
He saw poor George as but his darkest self
And all the possibility of the dark that he feared,
And so he struck, and struck down that darkest self,
And what is awful is that I must remember
That all my Lilburn wanted, after all—

JEFFERSON: Yes, there's your female fondness back again!

LUCY: Oh, it's not fondness to try to understand.

JEFFERSON: To understand? You mean, rather, to com-
                                   pound the crime.
LUCY: Compound the crime? Why, that's what you
                                   have done.
And do, for in your rejection you repeat the crime.
Over and over, and more monstrous still,
For what poor Lilburn did in exaltation of madness
You do in vanity—yes, Meriwether is right.
No, worse, you do it in fear—

JEFFERSON: What fear?
For whatever my failings, I feared no man.

LUCY: Yes, one.

JEFFERSON: Who?

LUCY: His name is Jefferson.
I mean yourself. I mean the deepest fear.
Yes, when you had learned in that report from Kentucky
What evil was possible even in the familial blood,
Your fear began, the fear you had always denied, the fear
That you—even you—were capable of all.
And so in that consanguinity, still to deny
The possibilities of self,
Even in the moment when you claimed that Lilburn
Had robbed you of your hope of human good,
In vanity and virtue and your fear,
You struck. You struck Lilburn down—and yet strike
Poor Lilburn down, and over and over again, the axe
Falls. The axe falls, and you cast him forth in the fire,
And the fire flares red on your face where the sweat is.
And as George was to Lilburn, so Lilburn is to you,
And as innocence was all Lilburn wanted, it is all
You yourself want, or have wanted. But, Brother,
If you would assume the burden of innocence—and dear
                                                   Brother,
I must say to you now, for it comes now strangely to me to
                                                   say it,
That the burden of innocence is heavier than the burden of
                                                   guilt—

But what I mean to say, if you would assume the burden of
innocence,
If you would begin now your innocence, you must take
His hand—

JEFFERSON: Yes, take it to congratulate him!

LUCY: It's not for him that I would have you do it.
There's nothing for him that a hand reached out could
do now.
It's for yourself—

JEFFERSON: To take it, and the blood slick on it?

LUCY: What if there's blood? We had hoped to escape
complicity,
You and I, dear Brother. But we have seen the unfolding
Of Time and complicity, and I, even in my love,
And in the milk of my breast, was in guilty involvement,
And my son died. And you, even in your aspiration,
Could prime the charge for our poor Meriwether.
And this is why in our best gifts we could give
Only the worst. It is because my love and your aspiration
Could not help but carry some burden of ourselves,
And to be innocent of that burden, at last,
You must take his hand, and recognize, at last,
That his face is only a mirror of your possibilities,

And recognize that you
Have deeper need of him than he of you,
For whatever hope we have is not by repudiation,
And whatever health we have is not by denial,
But in confronting the terror of our condition.
All else is a lie.

JEFFERSON: Yes, Meriwether said I lied,
But long since I had lost the strength for that lie,
But cannot yet find the strength to endure without it,
But can affirm my need only in the curse and rejection
Of him who had robbed me of the comfort of the lie.
I am tired. There must be a way to quietness.

LUCY: My Brother, I am ignorant and weak,
I failed in the world, and I feared darkness.
My heart was sick in the dark land I had come to,
And backward over the mountains, toward some joy and
                               innocence, my heart yearned.
But if there can be truth in ignorance,
And if there can ever be strength in sad weakness,
Believe, Brother, that I have told you the only way.

JEFFERSON: If I believe you, what is left for me?
What's left, at least, of the hope I once had?

LUCY: All's left. At least, all's left that's worth the having.

JEFFERSON: Well, what's worth having? What for me,

at least,

If all I dreamed was emptiness, and the dream
Itself was, as you say, but a reflex of my vanity?

LUCY: Your dream, my dear Brother, was noble. I'd not

deny that.

If there was vanity, fear, and deceit, in its condition,
What of that? For we are human, and must work
In the shade of our human condition. The dream remains.
But my dear Brother, if your dream
Was noble, there's a nobler yet to dream.
It will be nobler because more difficult and cold
In the face of the old cost of the human redemption,
And knowledge of that cost is, in itself, a kind of redemption.

JEFFERSON: I think I know what you would say to me.
One day I wrote to Adams, long ago—
To Adams, my old enemy and friend, that gnarled great-

ness, long ago.

I wrote to him, and said
That the dream of the future is better than the dream of

the past.

Now I should hope to find the courage to say
That the dream of the future is not
Better than the fact of the past, no matter how terrible.
For without the fact of the past we cannot dream the future.

I think I begin to see the forging of the future.

It will be forged beneath the hammer of truth

On the anvil of our anguish. We shall be forged

Beneath the hammer of truth on the anvil of anguish.

It would be terrible to think that truth is lost.

It would be worse to think that anguish is lost, ever.

GEORGE: I was lost in the world, and the trees were tall.

I was lost in the world, and the dark swale heaved.

I was lost in my anguish, and I did not know the reason.

JEFFERSON: Reason? My son, we have been lost in

the dark.

And I was lost, who had dreamed there was a light.

How could I show to you now the light of reason

When I had lost it when your blood ran out,

And the flame thirsted?

But we are condemned to reach yet for a reason.

We are condemned to some hope. And there may be yet

A reason that your anguish, and my own vanity,

Can hope, at last, to find.

To find? Oh, no!

To think to find it as a given condition of man

Would be but to repeat, I now see,

My old error. I have suffered enough for that.

Oh, no, if there is to be reason, we must

Create the possibility
Of reason, and we can create it only
From the circumstances of our most evil despair.
We must strike the steel of wrath on the stone of guilt,
And hope to provoke, thus, in the midst of our coiling

darkness

The incandescence of the heart's great flare.
And in that illumination I should hope to see
How all creation validates itself,
For whatever you create, you create yourself by it,
And in creating yourself you will create
The whole wide world and gleaming West anew.

Dance back the buffalo, the shining land!
Our grander Ghost Dance dance now, and shake the feather.
Dance back the morning and the eagle's cry.
Dance back the Shining Mountains, let them shine!
Dance into morning and the lifted eye.
Dance into morning past the morning star,
And dance the heart by which we have lived and died.
My Louisiana, I would dance you, though afar!

For nothing we had,
Nothing we were,
Is lost.
All is redeemed,
In knowledge.

But knowledge is the most powerful cost.
It is the bitter bread.
I have eaten the bitter bread.
In joy, I would end.

R. P. W.: We must consider those who could not end in joy.
Take George all huddled for the senseless axe,
Or old Aunt Cat, whom the Lord let live too long.
Take poor Laetitia, who could never know
The truth she longed for, what her story meant.
Take Meriwether in the moonlight calling
For water, water, in the hour of his bitter repudiation.
Take Lilburn counting slow, and longing for the hot lead.
And Isham—but for Isham we don't know.
His lie about his brother's death availed
Exactly nothing—if he had meant it to.
Accessory they named him, and the jury
Called for the rope, and Isham lay in jail.

The day drew on, and his appetite, no doubt,
Declined, and hog and hominy had lost
Their pristine savor, like the Bible's salt.
The day drew on, drew near, but never came.
The dawn broke fair to make the holiday,
But sport was lacking—sing or drink or fight
But ne'er a rope to stretch: "Aw, hell, git home."
Yes, the rope swings idle, for Isham's up and gone.

But the Commonwealth, aroused, will not be balked.
Far off in Frankfort, in the Capitol,
Old Shelby dipped his quill and wrote it fair,
The big reward, five hundred dollars, gold,
For Isham, quick or dead. That ought to fetch him.
But didn't. He's long gone, he's made his tracks
Down Mississippi, or the Arkansas.
He didn't break that jail to mope and tarry,
For Little Ishey had a prejudice
Against all hemp and hanging and bad dreams.
So busted jail—

ISHAM: No, I ne'er busted jail.
But I might have done it if I figured how,
For I lay in jail a-feared because they'd hang me,
Ashamed of being scared, and knowing, too,
They ought to hang me, for I killed my brother.
But old Thomas Terry—he guarded jail and me—
Old Tom, one night he came and said real soft,
"Was you to hit me now, and leave me lay,
You mought git off. You'll find a hoss all saddled
Down in the willow thicket. Hit's my hoss."
"Your horse—" I said. And him: "The hell whose hoss!
Hit's hoss or rope, and son, you better ride."
"You mean—" I said, "—you mean you'll let me go?"
And him: "Why, son, lak ever-body knows,
You warn't the one what brung the meanness on."

But I near yelled: "I killed my Bubber, I killed him!"
But couldn't yell, nor speak. He laughed, and said:
"I seen 'em hang, you wouldn't lak hit, son."
And said: "I'm gittin old, don't hit me hard."
I didn't hit him hard. Just like he said.

R. P. W.: And rode away and waited for the end.

ISHAM: I rode away, and threw my name away.
I wasn't Isham what had killed his brother.
I wasn't nothing, not nobody now,
Like something wind will blow, or blow right through,
Like thistle-fuzz or a scarecrow on a stick.
I said: "I'm nothing, and nothing ever happened."
I said: "I'll ride, and never have no name."
And rode.

       And rode, but knew the one durn thing
A man can't do is throw himself away.
He can't just squeeze it up inside his hand
And throw away his name and days and time
And all the things inside his head, and go.
So everything was there. *I* rode with *me,*
But kept on saying how I wasn't me.
But in the dark I said: "Oh, Lord, I'm me!"
And then New Orleans, and the time came on.

R. P. W.: So that is true?—the tale the riflemen
Brought back and told the homefolks and recorded

When they had finished that big turkey-shoot
With Andy Jackson at the cotton bales?
Yeah, every bastard got a turkey there!
It wasn't like a turkey-shoot back home
At forty paces, and the turkey's head
Is not a barn-door when it bobs up quick
Behind the log and then is down again,
And that split second is your only chance
To plug your pellet where the eye had been.
No, this was different, Andy gave the party
And any fool could get a turkey here,
And womenfolks or brats might done as well,
With every turkey-gobbler six feet tall
And gobbling slow and footing on the green,
A-walking at you, red and puffed with gobbling,
With drums a-gobbling too, to set the time,
And nary a log to duck the head behind.

ISHAM: Durn fools, durn fools—to see 'em march so pretty,
With red clothes shining like a wedding was,
Just marching at you like they never cared
You aimed to kill 'em and to leave 'em lay.
They marched so pretty, that's what made you mad,
To be so brave like all you did was nought,
And any dying you could give was nothing,
They'd spit on it, and you, and keep on marching.
It made you mad, because you knew down deep

How scared you'd be if you was marching there.
It made you mad, and so you'd lay your aim
On one, and take the fool, and load your Betsy.
Just take it easy, count your powder right.

Then we were yelling at the cotton bales.
I jumped up high and waved my cap and yelled.
I yelled for glory, how we killed and slayed,
We'd show those fools, just let 'em march again,
And yelling, too, because they marched so pretty
Who came across the waters far away
To march so pretty till the plug bit home,
And yelling, too, for something deep inside me,
Like I was back with folks a minute, maybe,
And then it hit me.

                    Some durn fool out yonder,
Some last durn fool that risked his hide to do it,
Out there with all his kind all dead around him,
Takes time to load and shoot just one more time
Back at those cotton bales. 'Twas me he found.
Right in the chest, a red-coat musket-ball.

A rifle plug like ours, it's small and true
And goes in easy, not much blood comes out.
But muskets, hell—if you can hit a thing,
It gives a *chunk*, it knocks a hole, and messy.

It made a mess of me. The blood came out.
Somebody held my head to give me water.
He looked, and sudden stared, and said: "Be durn."

They knew me, Isham, and they named my name.
Folks from back home, come traveling all that way
To kill some red-coats and to hold my head
While I was dying, and they named my name.
I died right easy while they named my name
Like they forgave me, even if I killed my brother.

R. P. W.: And now in the Smithland courthouse, on the
                                        indictment
The Commonwealth as Plaintiff had drawn for murder,
We find endorsed:
                    The same Plaintiff
                        against
                  Isham Lewis Defendant
          Ordered that this suit be abated by
          The death of the defendant.
                                    That is all.
It is abated. All is abated now.

It is abated, and your brother now
Sleeps in his dusty triumph, all alone.
No, not alone, his mother sleeping nigh.
But there is no communication between them.

No voice, no tread intrudes on the common silence,
And the jay's call is the index of indifference.
Nobody comes. You cannot find the graves.
I've tried, but the ferocious tangle of blackberry
Is sovereign on the spot. Nobody comes.

AUNT CAT: I come, one time. Long age and time ago,
Afore they up and taken me away,
Back to Virginny, whar they let me die.
The Lawd let me die, Who done let me live too long,
And ever-thing tromps sweetness out yore heart.
Oh, Lil. Oh, Chile. I come and seen the ground
Whar you laid down and bled yore gore away.
Oh, Lil, oh, Chile, I come and seen and said:
"Whar is my Lil? He ain't beneath this ground.
Oh, it ain't Lil what puked my milk away.
Oh, it ain't Lil what done all he could do
To not be Lil and made the people sad.
Oh, it ain't Lil, hit's some mean stranger sly
To come and steal yore name and face away
And blame on Lil how time and world is awful
And weevil in the meal and spring run dry
And yearth will shake and all the hills fall down
And folks don't love nobody—hit ain't my Lil."

Fer then I knowed whar my Lil come to stay,
Lak comin home and git inside the door.

My Lil, he come inside my heart to stay
And hang his hat and taken ease, and all
My heart git singin and the fire dance bright.
Sing, "Lil!" Sing: "Lil, my Leetle Baby-Bear."
Sing: "Lil, won't nothin come and git you now.
Raw-Head, Raw-Head, doan come my baby nigh.
Chile safe in Mammy's heart, and shet the door.
Let Ole Wind blow, and let Ole Time go by."
Chile safe asleep. I knowed the place he lay.

R. P. W.: The actual body of Lilburn, or what remains,
Lies sixty paces, more or less, beyond
The ruin of the Lewis house, about northwest.
Last year—in 1951—I went
My last time there. It was December then,
And under paleness of the lemon light
The heart of earth drew inward, and was still.
Under that hollow and fastidious light
Some far voice speaking, or a dog's bark,
Carried with calm and frosted ceremony
Its sad perfection past the field and farm.
Past pond and stubblefield the sound persists.
It persists in that cold indifferency of light.
It ravels upward in emptiness of light.
By hedgerow clump, woods-edge, and shaded slope
A little snow clings, longing for the night.
Tonight the heel will ring on the earth like iron.

Now under the lemon light we move,

My father and I,

Through the landscape of his early experience.

We pass the land where once stood the house of his first light.

No remnant remains. The plow-point has passed where the

sill lay.

The plow had passed long years before my birth.

The old house, square, set on limestone, by cedars, that I,

In the mind, see, is not a house I have seen.

I do not know what hope or haplessness there

Inhabited once. The house is a fiction of human

Possibility past. We whirl past the spot it held.

The grave of my father's father is lost in the woods.

The oak-root has heaved down the headstone.

I should not know how to come there. Who knows now?

My father himself has, no doubt, lost that orientation.

He says: "About this time, about December,

I recollect my father, how he'd take

Some yellow percoon, just the root, and mash it,

And bark of prickly ash, and do the same,

And cram it in a gallon jug, with whisky."

"What for," I said, "—to make a kind of drink?"

"Why, no," he said, "it's medicine to take.

He'd set the jug near three months on a shelf.

To wait and make the medicine come true.

And spring came on, and then he'd call us boys—

All boys, we were a house of boys he had—

And line us up and give it, morn and night."
"What for?" I said. And he: "Why, Son, I reckon
It's old-folks talk, but then they held it true,
How in the spring you had to thin the blood.
My father said how winter thicked boys' blood
And made 'em fit for devilment, and mean.
But he'd sure fix it, whisky and percoon.
Percoon was bitter. It would wry your tongue."
"Percoon, what's that?" I said. And he: "Why, Son,
It's just some sort of plant they called percoon."
"But what's it like?" I said. And he: "Why, Son,
I just don't recollect. But it's percoon."

And so we passed that land and the weight of its mystery.
We passed the mystery of years and their logic,
And my father and I, we sat in our common silence.
And I have been a strayer and stranger in many nations.
I have been stranger in my bed, at night.
I have been stranger when the waiter turned away for

                                 my order.

I have been stranger at the breaking of bread.
I have been stranger at the monstrous conversation of ocean,
And when the pretty child laid a hand on my knee.
I have, in other words, shared the most common
Human experience, which makes all mankind one,
For isolation is the common lot,
And paradoxically, it is only by

That isolation that we know how to name
The human bond and thus define the self.

We moved through the lemon light. And there was Smithland.
No, not Sam Clemens' town now, after all.
Sure, there's the jail and courthouse, and the river,
And Smithland yet is no metropolis:
Pop. 501, the highway sign confesses.
But where the slab now cuts the town in two
A traffic signal jangles red and green,
And paint is on the houses, and new stores,
And gas pumps are a rash that's worse than measles.
And Ford and Plymouth vie to make you happy,
And money jingles in the local jeans.
That's fine. I don't begrudge such solvency,
And who's to blame if there's some correlation
Between it and the dark audit of blood
In some Korean bunker, at the midnight concussion?
Yes, who's to blame? For in the great bookkeeping
Of History, what ledger has balanced yet?
And every entry is a scrawl of blood.
So why blame Smithland? Why blame Mr. Boyle?
In any case, Boyle's not at home today—
Down in Paducah, sure, for Christmas shopping.
Garage gapes wide. No smoke is in his chimney,
But white and snug the house shines in the sun.

I enter the barn lot. I see the new difference.
The barn may sag some yet, but in the bright,

Cold sun the cattle stand. He's raising whiteface now.
They stare at you with noble stupidness.
They stare with an Olympian disdain,
For you're just one of that crank, dwarfish crew
Born to bring corn and spread it for the gods.
The jaws move slow. The bright drool drips in sun,
And under glossy flanks the fat flesh bulges
With deep delight of being flesh, for flesh
Is its own blessing and nobility.

But I'm not here to gloat on fattening steers
Or envy Mr. Boyle's new prosperousness.

Why am I here? Some need has drawn me, but I
Can't name its name, or see the face it wears.
Not yet. But there's the bluff. I'd better climb.
Strange now, today it doesn't look so high.
Not like it did the first time when I came—
July it was—and I damned the heat and briar,
Saw-vine, love-vine, and rose, then clambered through
The tall, hot gloom of oak and ironwood,
Where grapevine, big as boas, had shagged and looped
Jungle convolvement and visceral delight.
For that's the way I had remembered it.
But no, it's not like that. At least, not now,
And never was, I guess, but in my head.
There is some thicket, yes, and grapevine, sure,
But scraggly-thin and hanging like it's tired

From trees gone leafless now, and not so tall.
So I'm prepared for what I find up yonder:
The ruin all shrunken to a little heap
Of stone that grass and earth pre-empt again.
And those fine beech trees that I'd celebrated—
They just aren't there at all, and all I find
Are piddling shag-barks, walnuts, two or three,
And two oaks, scrub to middling, not to brag on.
So winter makes things small. All things draw in.

But worse than that. I had plain misremembered,
Or dreamed a world appropriate for the tale.
One thing, however, true: old *obsoleta*
Had reared that day, and swayed against the sun
To scare me, like that sort of thing will scare you.
Well, not today. He's keeping home this weather,
Down in the rocks, I reckon, looped and snug
And dark as dark: in dark the white belly glows,
And deep behind the hog-snout, in that blunt head,
The ganglia glow with what cold dream is congenial
To fat old *obsoleta*, winter-long.

Today he sleeps in earth's dark inwardness.
All things draw inward with the winter's will,
And over the earth here, on the fallen leaves,
The snow lies thin and pure, and I stand
Amid the brown leaves and snow. I lift up my eyes

Beyond the bluff and the flat land farther
To where the river gleams. Its gleam is cold.
And I think of another bluff and another river.
I think of another year and another winter.
I think of snow on the brown leaves, and below
That other bluff, how cold and far was light on that
                                    northern river.

I think how her mouth and mine together
Were cold on the first kiss. Sparsely, snow
Descended among the black trees. We kissed in the cold
Logic of hope and need. It was not joy.
Later, the joy. Or if not joy, the keen
Appetitive spur and that delicious delusion.
Who is to name delusion when the flesh shakes?
So in this other year, by another river,
Deep in the world of winter, snow on the brown leaves,
Far in Kentucky there, I raised my eyes
And thought of the track a man may take through Time,
And how our hither-coming never knows the hence-going.
Since then new ice on gutters and by pond-edge.
Since then I have made new acquaintance with snow on
                                    the brown leaves.
Since then I have made new acquaintance with the nature
                                    of joy.

I stood on the bluff and stared over the flat land to the river,
And I thought how men had moved on that broad flood,
The good, the bad, the strong, the weak, all men

The drawn, the driven, the fortunate, the feckless,
All men, a flood upon the flood, and I,
In that cold light, was impelled to apostrophize:
    "O you who have on your broad bosom borne
      Man and man's movement, and endured the oar,
      Keel-pole and paddle, sweep and the paddle-wheel,
      And suffered the disturbance of the screw's bronze
                                blade,
      And tissued over that perpetual scarification
      With instant sweetness and the confident flow—
      You who have suffered filth and the waste of the
                           human establishment,
      Ordure of Louisville and the slick of oil,
      The drowned cow, swollen, from the mountain cove,
      And junk jammed on the sand bar in the sun—
      I take you now as image and confirmation
      Of that deep flood that is our history,
      Of that deep flood that makes each new day possible
      And bears us westward to the new land.
      I take you as the image and confirmation
      Of some faith past our consistent failure, and the
                           filth we strew."

But even as I experienced this mood,
I knew that though the great river might be
Image, it could not be confirmation,
For even the grandeur of Nature may not be

Our confirmation. It is image only.

There is, indeed, the bickering glitter of waters sun-bit
to glory.

There is the taciturnity of stone black at the massif's jut
of noblest exposure,

Beyond the bloom-gaud of cirque, and the balsam's silence.

There is the wing-whistle of bomb-plunge of gannet, and
the moonlit unwhisper of owl-swoop.

And there is, always, the philosophic peace of a certain
pasture at evening, not seen since boyhood,

But whatever the gleam of massive magnificence or
glimmer of shy joy

May be, it can only resemble the moon

And is but mirror to the human heart's steadfast and
central illumination.

If there is glory, the burden, then, is ours.

If there is virtue, the burden, then, is ours.

And so I thought of the dead beneath my feet.

I thought of Lilburn on his mountain here,

Who brought no light into the dark, and so died.

And Meriwether dead in Tennessee,

Who had brought light to the dark, but died in darkness.

I thought of Lilburn on his mountain here,

And thought of another mountain, far away,

In Albemarle, where Lilburn's kinsman sleeps.

For they are kinsmen, and so I then thought

Of all who had come down the great river and are
Nameless, or if we know their names, then what
Is the truth we know? What if
We know the names of the niggers by the wall,
Who hunkered there and moaned? Yes, we know each name,
The age, and sex, and price, from the executor
Who listed all to satisfy the court:
Towit Ceolio one hundred and fifty dollars
William one hundred and Ten dollars Frank
four hundred and thirty-five dollars, et cetera.
But that is all—no face, no form, no wish of the heart.

Yes, that is all, and thus we know the names
Of those who went with Meriwether west
And lay on night-mats in rain, lulled in the immoderate
                                        utterance of ocean.
We know their names, and how all heard the ocean.
We know that much, but what is any knowledge
Without the intrinsic mediation of the heart?

They returned to St. Louis. Were mustered out. Took pay.
They stared at the strange new faces, and are gone.
Took pay, and stepped into the encroachment of shadow.

The years go by, but on some village bench,
Or in some grog-shop where the candle winks
And stutters on fat foulness of the fumes,
The gaffer leans, befogged by drink or age,

Daft with the last dazzlement of recollection,
And strikes his knee, or strikes the table-top,
And says, "God-durn, I seen hit, I was thar!"
And they: "Hell, Pap, shet up, you're drunk agin."
And he: "God-durn, I tell ye, I was thar!"

Yes, Pap, you saw it. We believe you, Pap.
Yes, you were there and saw it, for we, too,
Were there, and heard the mountain like a bell,
Lonely, boom, and heard the night-boom of ocean.
We heard the mutineer scream, and we felt, when the lash bit.
We stood at the cotton bales, and yelled for glory.
And we, too, had grooved the uneasy Atlantic to march
                                        toward death at the bales.
We marched to the iterative regularity of drums and lay
                                        down on foreign earth.
We have lifted the meat-axe in the elation of love and
                                        justice.
We have hunkered by the wall, and could not pray.
We have ground the gourd in the bucket and called for water,
For there was no water. We have seen the great bear die.
We have seen a small boy, wide-eyed, stand on the
                                        hearthstone
And accept, from his father's hand, the bitter dose of percoon.
The hearthstone is gone whereon he once stood.

We have yearned in the heart for some identification
With the glory of the human effort, and have yearned

For an adequate definition of that glory.
To make that definition would be, in itself,
Of the nature of glory. This is not paradox.
It is not paradox, but the best hope.

It is the best hope, because we have,
Each, experienced what it is to be men.
We have lain on the bed and devised evil in the heart.
We have stood in sunlight and named the bad thing good
                                    and the good thing bad.
We have stumbled into the act of virtue and caught only
                                    from the tail of the eye
The flicker of joy, like a wing-flash in thicket.

But we must argue the necessity of virtue:

In so far as man has the simplest vanity of self,
There is no escape from the movement toward fulfillment.
And since all kind but fulfills its own kind,
Fulfillment is only in the degree of recognition
Of the common lot of our kind. And that is the death of vanity,
And that is the beginning of virtue.

The recognition of complicity is the beginning of innocence.
The recognition of necessity is the beginning of freedom.
The recognition of the direction of fulfillment is the death
                                    of the self,

And the death of the self is the beginning of selfhood.
All else is surrogate of hope and destitution of spirit.

And so I stood on the headland and stared at the river
In the last light of December's, and the day's, declension.
And the river declared its cold gleam beyond the flat land.
I thought of the many dead and the places where they lay.
I looked at the shrunken ruin, and at the trees leafless,
And the wild vine leafless, and below the bluff at the barn-lot.
The winter makes things small. All things draw in.
It is strange how that shift of scale may excite the heart.

From an undifferentiated impulse I leaned
Above the ruin and in my hand picked up
Some two or three pig-nuts, with the husk yet on.
I put them in my pocket. I went down.

I was ready to go down, and perhaps never
Come back, for I did not know what here remained,
For me, at least; and to this day have not
Gone back; but hold, in my heart, that landscape.
I went down the bluff, and crossed the evening barn-lot.
I opened the sagging gate, and was prepared
To go into the world of action and liability.
I had long lived in the world of action and liability.
But now I passed the gate and entered a world
Sweeter than hope in that confirmation of late light.

I walked down to the car where my father had been **waiting**.
He woke from his cold drowse, and yawned, and said,
"You finished what you climbed up there for, Son?"
And I said: "Yes, I've finished. Let's go home."

Page 39

In 1785 the commission appointed to superintend the construction of a capitol in Richmond, Virginia, appealed to Jefferson for advice. He describes, in his autobiography, his response to this request. "Thinking it a favorable opportunity of introducing into the state an example of architecture in the classic style of antiquity, and the Maison Quarrée of Nismes, an ancient Roman temple, being considered as the most perfect model existing of what may be called Cubic architecture, I applied to M. Clerisseau, who had published drawings of the antiquities of Nismes, to have me a model of the building made in stucco, only changing the order from Corinthian to Ionic, on account of the difficulty of the Corinthian capitals. . . . To adapt the exterior to our use, I drew a plan for the interior, with the apartments necessary for legislative, executive, and judiciary purposes; and accommodated in their size and distribution to the form and dimensions of the building. These were forwarded to the directors in 1786, and were carried into execution." It was not until the next year—in March of 1787—that Jefferson saw the actual building at Nîmes. In a letter to the Comtesse de Tesse, a cousin of Lafayette, Jefferson delineates, somewhat whimsically, his grand architectural passion: "Here I am, Madam, gazing whole hours at the Maison Quarrée, like a lover at his mistress. The stocking weavers and silk spinners around it consider me a hypochondriac Englishman about to write with a pistol the last chapter of his history. This is the second time I have been in love since I left Paris. The first was with a Diana at the Chateau de Laye-Epinaye in Beaujolais, a delicious morsel of sculpture by M. A. Slodtz. This, you will say, was in rule, to fall in love with a female beauty; but with a house! it is out of all precedent."

Page 99

The passage on the Annus Mirabilis is drawn from the following letter:
"Many things conspired to make the year 1811 the *annus mirabilis* of the West. During the earlier months, the waters of many of the great rivers overflowed their banks to a vast extent, and the whole country was in many parts covered from bluff to bluff. Unprecedented sickness followed. A spirit of change and recklessness seemed to pervade the very inhabitants of the forest. A countless multitude of squirrels, obeying some great and universal impulse, which none can know but the Spirit that gave them being, left their reckless and gambolling life and their ancient places of retreat in the North, and

were seen pressing forward by tens of thousands in a deep and solid phalanx to the South. No obstacles seemed to check their extraordinary and concerted movement. The word had been given them to go forth, and they obeyed it, though multitudes perished in the broad Ohio, which lay in their path. The splendid comet of that year long continued to shed its twilight over the forests, and as autumn drew to a close, the whole valley of the Mississippi, from the Missouri to the Gulf, was shaken to its centre by continued earthquakes."

C. J. Latrobe, *The Rambler in North America,*
Vol. 1 (New York, 1835)

I am indebted to Miss Eudora Welty for calling my attention to this account.

Page 136

We the subscribers being called by the Coroner of this County of Livingston and St of Ky to hold an inquest on the Dead body of Jimmy a Chicisaw Indian in the house of James Levy in this town of Eddyville having examined the body of the said Jimmy do find the said Jimmy received several wounds in his head some of which appeared to have been made by strokes of a Club or Clubs in one place on his head the Scull seemed indented one wound in his head was about five inches long another about three inches long at right angles from the other those were apparently made by two or more strokes beside which we found one considerable burned spot on his back his nose was badly hurt we find the deceased was badly kicked about his face by means of all which wounds the said Indian has lost his life and that the wounds were given by Ruben Cook and Isaac Ferguson who are now in Gaol in this Town

Page 136

Com of Ky L C to wit

Whereas a Jury having been legaly summoned and met this 12 day of September 1804 to Enquire of the Death of A Negroe Man named Jack the property of John Sharp and find the following facts to wit Charles Jones being sworn deposet and saith that on Saturday the eighth of Sept as he was riding to Eddyville on the main road to to that place and about a mile or thereabouts from the s^d place he heard several blows that appeared to be like the striking of a lazy horse with club and a rusling among the stone and gravel like that of a cart or waggon and upon a nearer approach he saw a negro man running toward me with hands tied behind and was very much fatigued and worried he appeared to have down in the dirt as his hair was very dirty and his mouth open which I supposed was occationed by the running and beating which he had received. I saw large man on horse back following him with a Club in his hand and beating him every opportunity in a very inhuman manner. I called to the man and said for God sake to spare his life for he could not stand it to go far in that way but all he said as he past me was goodbye or how da do sir I turned around and look't after him untill they were both out of sight and the man was still beating him as far as I could see and on my return from Eddyville the same day about the middle of the afternoon tracked them for several miles I think about five it appeared that the negro had ran all the way except in one place about ten or fifteen yards and when I saw that he had left running I expected to have found him dead but not finding him I took his track and went on about one mile farther into the Barrens where I found a place where the grass was beat down for a considerable space here again expected to have found him dead as there were a number of Clubs lying about the place and some blood and which I had seen in number of the other places as I had followed the track which supposed came from the negro—I look't about the place in the barrens before mentioned expecting to find his body but being unwell I quit the place and went home and on Tuesday following I heard of a negro being found dead in the barrens I enquired whereabouts and was informed it was at or about the same place where I had seen the Clubs and the grass beat down and further saith not.

March 19, 1812

The grand jury returned sev
presentments and disch^d.

Lilburn Lewis appeared in court in discharge of his recognizance and the grand having found an indictment against him and Isham Lewis for murder and the said Isham L. being in court they were ordered into the custody of the sheriff Whereupon the Defendants by their council moved the court to hear the evidence upon an application to admit the prisoners to bail Tomorrow morning at 9 o'clock and upon the application of the defendants to recognize the witnesses to appear on Tomorrow. Lilburn Lewis, Archibald Cannon, William Dyer Ackn^d themselves indebted in $200 each conditioned to appear here tomorrow

Ordered that Court adjourned to tomorrow 9 o'clock

Page 165

In the name of God Amen This my last Will Ac. 1st It my desire that all my Just debts be paid and then my property both real and personal be equally divided between my children Jane W Lewis, Lucy I Lewis, Lilburn L Lewis, Elizabeth Lewis, Robert Lewis and James R. Lewis reserving to my beloved but cruel wife Latitia G. Lewis her Lawful part of said property during her natural life. 2nd It my desire that my beloved father Charles L Lewis be possessed of the riding horse which I purchased of Hurley my rifle and shot bag during his natural life also my walking cane and that my beloved sisters Martha C Lewis Lucy B Lewis and Nancy M Lewis may be comforted from the perquisites of sd estate by my executors as providence may require or in other words so as to do my children and themselves entire Justice. 3rd I do hereby constitute my beloved father Charles L Lewis the revd Wm Woods near Salem Saml C. Harknes James MCawley and Archd Ferguson my executors whoom I must remind that Huey F. Delaney has received a fee from me for the prosecution in a Trespass against James Rutter senr, James Rutter Jr James Young and Thomas Terry given under my hand this and revoking all and every other will heretofore made, nineth day of Aprl. Eighteen hundred and Twelve   Lilburn Lewis

NB. My dog Nero I do hereby bequeath to my beloved father L. D.

Rocky Hill Aprl 9th 1812. Mr. James MCawley I have fallen a victim to my beloved but cruel Letitia I die in the hope of being united to my other wife in heaven take care of this will and come here that we may be decently buried Adew—L. Lewis

NB. Within this inclosure myself and brother requests be entered in the same coffin and in the same ~~ground~~ grave

Rocky Hill Apr 10th 1812 my beloved but cruel Letitia receive this as a pledge of my forgiveness to your connections the day of Judgment is to come I owe you no malice but die on account of your Absence and my dear little son James Adieu my love

Lilburn Lewis

Livingston County SLC May County Court 1812
The within will was proven to be the handwriting of Lilburn Lewis by William Rice James MCawley and Lilburn Lewis sen^r and ordered to be recorded

Test Enoch Prince

Page 171

We of the Jury are of the opinion that Lilburn Lewis Did murder him self on the 10th Day of April 1812 on his own plantation and Isham Lewis ~~first~~ present and acessary ~~axeesary~~ to the Murder

Wm Rutter fore Mⁿ.

Jury   upon oath

Isham Lewis before the and saith that him self and Lilbourne
Lewis agreed to present a gun at each others breast and fire
at a word with an intention of killing each other—but that
Lilbourne in in trying an experiment accidentially shot him
self dead

April 11th 1812

Sworn to

before_____John Darrah

Coroner L C

Page 177

The details of the Lewis and Clark expedition are drawn from
their journals, especially the entries for the following dates:

1804: February 11 and October 14.

1805: January 5, April 29, May 5, May 11, May 17, June 10,
July 2, July 4, August 16, August 20, September 22,
November 7.

1806: January 21.

The entry of July 4, 1805, discusses the great sound heard
in the mountains. The members of the expedition heard it on
various occasions, the single bell-like stroke or the succession
of sounds like the discharge of a battery of six-pounders at a
distance of about three miles. The same phenomenon had

been reported by the Pawnees and Ricaras in the Black Mountains, and I have read an account of such a sound in the mountains of Arkansas, given by Thomas Nuttall, a trained scientist, who published *A Journal of Travels into the Arkansas Territory during the Year 1819* (Philadelphia, 1881). An eminent geologist whom I have questioned informs me that science has no explanation of this phenomenon, and he himself is strongly inclined to doubt the veracity of the record. The explanation given Lewis and Clark by their French watermen was that the sound came from the bursting of rich lodes of silver confined in the bosom of the mountains.

Page 185

Meriwether Lewis died in what is now Lewis County, Tennessee, some seventy-five miles southwest of Nashville. His monument is a broken plinth, erected by the Legislature of Tennessee, in 1848. The inscriptions are as follows:

(*West face*)

Meriwether Lewis

Born near Charlottesville, Virginia, August 18, 1774

Died October 11, 1809, aged 35 years

(*South face*)

An officer of the Regular Army—Commander of the Expedition to the Oregon in 1803–1806—Governor of the

Territory of Louisiana—His melancholy death
occurred where this monument now
stands, and under which rest
his mortal remains.

(East face)

In the language of Mr. Jefferson: "His courage was undaunted;
his firmness and perseverance yielded to nothing but im-
possibilities; A rigid disciplinarian, yet tender as a
father of those committed to his charge; honest,
disinterested, liberal, with a sound under-
standing and a scrupulous fidelity
to truth."

(North face)

Immaturus obi; sed tu felicior annos
Vive meos, Bona Respublica! Vive tuos.

Page 195

From the time of the eighteenth century, when the white set-
tlers first broke in force across the mountains, there had been
occasional bursts of excitement among the Indians at the notion of a Messiah who would restore their old life. But after
the Civil War, when the Indians of the West were in the last
paroxysm of resistance and despair, the religion of the Ghost
Dance appeared. The founder—Jack Wilson to the whites and
Wovoka to the Indians—was a Paiute Indian, son of Tavibo
the prophet, born in Mason Valley, Nevada.

Wovoka was a dreamer and mystic who gave a dance to his people, and who on one occasion, at the time of a total eclipse of the sun, went into a trance and was taken to the other world where he saw God and all the beloved dead who were happy at their old sports and occupations in a land teeming with buffalo and elk. God told Wovoka that he must return and preach a gospel of love and peace, of industriousness and truth, and that if the Indians followed the gospel they would in the end enter into the blessed world. In Wovoka's own words: "When the sun died I went up to heaven and saw God and all the people who had died a long time ago. God told me to come back and tell my people they must be good and love one another, and not fight, or steal, or lie. He gave me this dance to give to my people."

The news of the promise swept over the West, and assumed many forms. There was, for instance, the notion among the Cheyennes, Arapaho, and other tribes that the new shining earth would come sliding from the West over the old worn-out earth, and that the living Indians would be lifted up and transported to it by the aid of the sacred dance feathers in their hair which would serve as wings. Some held that there would be a wall of fire before the New Earth to drive the whites away, and some held that there would be a great cataclysmic shaking of the old earth perhaps accompanied by a flood from which only the Indians would be saved to live in the shining land among the happy resurrected dead and the fat herds of buffalo. The Sioux, of course, did not wait for that moment, but took matters into their own hands with the outbreak of 1890.

As for the dance itself, it was circular, with a slow, dragging step, accompanied by song, interrupted now and then for exhortation or recitation by the medicine man. When a dancer began to show signs of the trance the medicine man would shake the eagle feather in front of the subject's eyes until the seizure had its full force and the dreamer fell down to enjoy his vision of the New Earth. Mothers sometimes brought toys or garments to give to dead children whom they might encounter in the trance.

For further information about the Ghost Dance, see *The Ghost-Dance Religion and the Sioux Outbreak of 1890*, by James Mooney, in the *Fourteenth Annual Report of the Bureau of Ethnology*, Part 2, and *The Pawnee Ghost Dance Hand Game*, by Alexander Lesser, New York, 1933.

Page 201

Monday the 20th March 1815

The same   Plaintiff

against

Isham Lewis   Defendant

Ordered that this suit abate by the

death of the defendant.*

* *On the back of the indictment for murder.*

January the 2ⁿᵈ 1813

Agreeable to an order of the Livingston County Court appointing us commissioners to appraise the negroes belonging to the estate of Lilburne Lewis dec^d and to allott Latetia G. Lewis widow of said Lilburne Lewis dec^d her third part of said negroes we met at the house of James Rutter sen^r on the day above mentioned and valued said negroes as follows Towit Ceolio one hundred and fifty dollars William one hundred and Ten dollars Mosley three hundred and Twenty five dollars Carter four hundred and thirty-five dollars Aggy three hundred and fifty dollars Isaac two hundred and seventy five dollars Patsy Two hundred and eighty five dollars Archie four hundred and seventy five dollars Mary two hundred and Twenty-five dollars we then proceeded to assign to the widow the following negroes Towit Ceolio William Frank an Usley [Mosley?] witness our hands this day and date above written

John Mott
S C Harknis   Comm^s
Joseph Rice

About the AUTHOR

Born in Guthrie, Kentucky, in 1905, Robert Penn Warren lived there until he was fifteen. He entered Vanderbilt University at the age of sixteen to study for a scientific career, but found the study of literature more interesting. Having graduated *summa cum laude,* he went to the University of California for his Master's Degree, then to Yale University, and in 1928 to Oxford as a Rhodes scholar.

Upon returning to the United States, Mr. Warren turned to teaching—first at Southwestern College, then at Vanderbilt University. In 1934 he went to Louisiana State University, where in addition to his teaching duties, he became one of the founders and editors of *The Southern Review,* one of our most distinguished literary magazines. From 1942 to 1950 he was Professor of English at the University of Minnesota, and in 1944–45 also served as Consultant in Poetry at the Library of Congress. Since 1951 he has been a member of the faculty of Yale University, where he divides his teaching time between the English Department and the Drama School.

Although he had already received a number of prizes for his poems, it was only in 1939 that Mr. Warren published his first novel, *Night Rider* (reissued by Random House in 1948), and won his first Guggenheim Fellowship. In 1943 came *At Heav-*

en's Gate and in 1946, *All the King's Men,* which won him the Pulitzer Prize and the Robert Meltzer Award of the Screenwriters Guild in 1949. His most recent novel, *World Enough and Time,* was published by Random House in 1950. Mr. Warren has also written three volumes of poetry and a short-story collection, *The Circus in the Attic,* in addition to many critical studies and textbooks.